**Star
Charting**

Practices

A series edited by Margret Grebowicz

Doing Nothing by James Currie
Fly-Fishing by Christopher Schaberg
Juggling by Stewart Lawrence Sinclair
Raving by McKenzie Wark
Riding by Pardis Mahdavi
Running by Lindsey A. Freeman
Star Charting by Bess Matassa
Taking Leave by Deborah Kapchan
Tomorrowing by Terry Bisson

Star
Charting

Bess Matassa

DUKE UNIVERSITY PRESS

Durham and London

2026

© 2026 DUKE UNIVERSITY PRESS

Project Editor: Bird Williams
Designed by A. Mattson Gallagher
Typeset in Untitled Serif and General Sans
by Copperline Book Services

Library of Congress Cataloging-in-Publication Data
Names: Matassa, Bess, author.
Title: Star charting / Bess Matassa.
Other titles: Practices.
Description: Durham : Duke University Press, 2026. | Series: Practices
Identifiers: LCCN 2025025472 (print)
LCC 2025025473 (ebook)
ISBN 9781478033141 (paperback)
ISBN 9781478029694 (hardcover)
ISBN 9781478061908 (ebook)
Subjects: LCSH: Matassa, Bess. | Astrology—Social aspects. | Zodiac. |
Tarot cards.
Classification: LCC BF1711. M455 2026 (print)
LCC BF1711 (ebook)
LC record available at https://lccn.loc.gov/2025025472
LC ebook record available at https://lccn.loc.gov/2025025473

Cover text handwritten by Bess Matassa.

To the anima in everything

Introduction

The Practice of Astrology

The stars saved my life.

Bottomed out in the throes of a psychological breakdown during my Saturn Return — a cosmic event that inspires reckoning — I nearly poofed myself from the planet. As I teetered on the edge of the subway platform, ready to roll onto the tracks, my life depended on the answer to one question: *Could I live with what lived inside of me?*

In astrological terms, what lived inside of me was on fire. My birth chart — the symbolic snapshot of the cosmos taken as each one of us enters it — contains an Aries stellium, a thick concentration of this sign's charge. The original big bang of the zodiac, the first fire sign of Aries invites us to strike a match and bring everything around us to life. I come from an ancestral line set ablaze. My maternal grandmother, thrice exorcised as a child, had once actually flared up beside the family poker table, courtesy of a lit Newport dropped into a housecoat pocket (she swore she'd quit). Her sister had suffered a far worse fate by flame: She blacked out and was incinerated in a boardinghouse bed.

As an adolescent, my own skin erupted into outbreaks of shiny red hives ("too much heat," according to the Eastern doctors). And from those red hots that smoldered on my surface, everything started to ignite. I branded daredevil boyfriends in the second and third degrees, goading them into incendiary acts of fire juggling and breathing. When my own hair caught in a candle while I bent over a bathroom sink in a cocaine-fueled frenzy, I just let it burn.

Like some kind of cannibalistic cardioverter, I was hell-bent on provoking life's pulse to beat faster. And by the time of my Saturn Return in my late twenties, I'd become a verb with no subject in sight. In the oft-cited concept championed by Carl Jung—one of the progenitors of "psychological astrology," a twentieth-century answer to more deterministic strains of studying the stars—until we make the unconscious within us conscious, we will collide with it in the world and call it fate. If my fate was on fire, I was finally ready to face it.

Guided by an astrologically inspired Jungian analyst during my breakdown, my crude form of power was ground up by the celestial body Pluto. A "higher octave" expression of Aries energy, Pluto is the planetary god who metal-detects both the matter we've exiled from our consciousness and the precious stuff we've clung on to at all costs. The heroic story I'd cultivated to keep myself safe got shredded, and my deepest fears about who I really was beneath all my bravado were laid bare: puny, pathetic, and destined to be pulverized.

Astrology became my headlamp in the darkness, and I mined mystical meaning for dear life. In the star-charted ecosystem that lived within me, every single element was infused with significance; nothing was arbitrary, out of place, or unworthy of love. Far from circumstantial or pathological, through the eyes of astrology my intensity was mythological instead. And with mythos and meaning, anything was endurable and, perhaps, even possible. My crisis issued an ultimatum to the heroics I'd always held close: If I said yes to the bigness that still lived within my birth chart, it would remember me to a world where I still mattered—and where my story was far from done.

At the heart of my expedition into my interior was the ultimate gift and challenge of this language of the stars: the chance to quit grasping *for* power and *against* powerlessness, and to actually start participating in the powers that were moving through me and all around me. The life forces that were mine but also so much more than just mine.

The Practice of Star Charting:
A Biodiversity of Being

Long before the stars saved my life, they had first brought me to it.

At age eleven, my hot little fire-sign hands clutched DK Publishing's *Parkers' Astrology* as I pored over the full-color pages packed with glossy images of the colors, cities, herbs, and animals corresponding to each zodiac sign. The world spilled its sparkle, and my everyday existence became an ongoing astrological treasure hunt. Determined to scratch 'n' sniff every archetype out in the wild, I hunted signs of the signs everywhere. Gemini's prism-like possibilities appeared in stick-on rhinestone earrings at the drugstore. Scorpio's excavation of the outmoded surfaced in thick charcoal face masks applied ceremoniously at sleepovers.

What I encountered through these scratch 'n' sniffs were astrology's fundamental tenets of archetypal resonance and energetic affinity. From Babylon onward, similar astrological symbols and associated meanings have sprung up spontaneously across cultures and have remained remarkably stable through time. This symbology has been inspired by our reciprocity with the cycles of the natural world and our felt experience of its four elements (fire, earth, air, water)—the omnipresent matter from which all stuff on earth is made. Astrology is the language in which existence speaks.

Astrology "works" because we are part of everything that surrounds us, it is part of us, and we are all part of something larger. This is the ancient, hermetic "as above, so below" precept not as a fancy metaphor but as living fact (as in "heaven is a place on earth" in the lyrics of Belinda Carlisle). The energetic current of Gemini, for example, is immanent; it already breathes its way through life. We lift it to the surface when we feel its presence in a person, place, or thing and recognize it by its Gemini name. The stick-on rhinestone earrings aren't merely symbolic representations of the sign's color-changing qualities—they *are* Gemini energy itself. And whether or not we're born under the Sun sign of Gemini or have Gemini planets placed in our birth charts (more on this soon), any one of us can stick on those stones and catch all kinds of light.

In my childhood scratch 'n' sniffs, I didn't actually need to understand how or why astrology worked, or how it came into the world, because it was already here and working—its essence emanated from everything around me and was instantly recognizable. This is the numinous potential of astrology as a revolutionary mode of apprehending the world. When we suspend our obsession with ferreting out the how and why of something, and soften our hunger to extract and impose meaning, we can become more curious about listening to and liberating inherent significance. Instead of pulling the pieces of an apparatus apart and asking them to explain themselves and prove their purpose, we start putting the fractured shards of this world back together where they belong. Understanding becomes an art of recognizing an already meaningful, magical universe.

This approach demystifies and redemocratizes divinity. When we return astrology to its original lineage as part of life itself—rather than holding it at analytical arm's length as something to be dissected, intellectualized, or even learned—we return it to all of us to enjoy and interpret, no matter our context or conditions. Astrology becomes a sacred process of participation through which we can remember and recover our original, intuitive knowing. Thus, we can transform it from an occult tool that's too often been kept hidden and hoarded by a select few and turn it back into the open secret we've shared with all of life, all along.

The psychological breakdown that birthed my career as a professional mystic was contemporaneous with the completion of my PhD. In my field of urban cultural geography, I was enamored of any method that kept me close to the ground: ethnography, embodiment, everyday practice. As I began offering astrological services to others, I was beckoned even closer down to earth, and any lingering traces of academia's conceptual distance quickly burned off. When reading birth charts, I was handling people's hearts in real time, and the magic had to meet the messy matter of life experience at every turn. With my feet firmly on the street, my first offering, called Street Signs, led people on astrological walking tours that brought their birth chart energies alive through New York City's landscape.

While I'm deeply indebted to the work of psychological astrologers like Liz Greene and Dane Rudhyar—among many other mystics and mediums of all stripes—my own astrological practice continues to thrive and evolve when it breathes through all forms of beingness rather than seeking to situate itself within a particular cohort of practitioners or field of study. The "field" is the fullest range of existence, unfiltered. And the "method" is to let more of this matter meet us and to call it by new names. Here, astrology becomes a poetic practice that pulses in concert with all kinds of creations: from the life-leaning-forward of Aries grass blades punching through the pavement cracks to the iridescent bubble-pop confections of Pisces Moon Carly Rae Jepsen.

From baby Bess astro-autodidact to post-Saturn-Return professional star charter, my astrological practice has always been born from the beauty of this original belief: Astrology is no different from life. It *is* life, and when wielded with wonder, it can give us even more life. Seen as synonymous with existence, astrology becomes a call to celebrate the soul of every speck and mini-shimmer that's got a spark. Quite simply, if you've lived through it, touched it, tasted it, there's an astrological name for it. And when we call things by their names and let them exist in all their beingness, we liberate them to become more of what they are already born to be.

This is the true alchemy of astrology used in service of evolution: to behold without analysis, explanation, or augmentation; to hold with love and to let live.

Collectively, we are experiencing a crisis of separation—born from barren ways of existing built on extraction, othering, and the abject denial of human complexity. We see it in cancel culture's refusal to acknowledge our capacity for reckoning, transformation, and redemption. It's in the haunted hierarchies of toxic masculinity and white supremacy. In the saturated media sight lines, which seem to show us everything while often leaving us with less than nothing. In our ceaseless march toward artificial intelligence without the commensurate growth of our emotional intelligence. In our self-imposed exile from the earth itself. And, most terrifyingly, in one ferocious fact: After centuries of so-called progress, we cannot stop killing each other.

As our crisis of separation has escalated, modern spirituality practices—and astrology, in particular—have proliferated, fueled by the human quest to find some scraps of meaning amidst the shrapnel and to try to remember that we all share something larger that might even be divine. We've begun to intuit, and rightfully so, that our challenges cannot be faced by employing the same methodologies and worldview that created them: ones that rely only on what we can see, touch, manipulate, and prove and that prize the trafficking of information at the cost of emotional experience. We need a new mythos, now more than ever. Stories with heart and guts that allow us to be both human and heroic.

Some of the astrological offerings that have emerged from our crisis are nuanced, while others are more like fast fixes: date-driven horoscopes, "what's your sign?" memes, and dating apps that promise star-studded soulmates at first swipe. At best, these offerings give us an expanded language for thinking about who we are and what we're up to on earth. At worst, they become akin to an astrological eugenics that keeps us safe in our separateness by deflecting blame and denying ownership of certain aspects of life. *He's such a Taurus, that's why he's so stubborn. . . . I'll never be with another Scorpio—toxic! . . . I've got to wait till Mercury retrograde ends to make plans. . . .*

As with all modes of meaning making, we suffer when we use astrology for determinism and event-based prediction at both ends of the fate–free-will spectrum. As either a fatalistic abdication of responsibility—where we shut our eyes tight and hope the stars align for a "good" future—or a rigid, rationalist exercise in figuring out exactly how astrology "works" so that we can strip it of its intuitive poetry and use it to control outcomes and mastermind our grand plans.

But astrology is neither a religious practice nor a scientific method. It is not the answer to our prayers nor even to our questions. Instead, when we let it live in the liminal space between fate and free will, this ancient romance language becomes a love letter to the anima in everything. It offers us a chance to respond to our current crisis of separation with the diversity of divinity, by beholding the astounding complexity inside ourselves, each other, and the world around us.

When we practice astrology, we shift from a who's-doing-what-to-whom universe of causality into an emergent landscape of collaboration with the weather conditions, which can actually give rise to change. We stop asking, *What's going to happen to me?* and start wondering, *What's happening here?* By shifting our inquiry and invigorating our compassion and curiosity, we become part of the world once again. Instead of pushing away certain expressions of life that might not be to our taste, we become omnivores of experience who metabolize every flavor, from the clarifying citrus of Libra to the fortifying bone stock of Capricorn. This is the practice that led me away from my duel-to-the-death attempt to eradicate the gnarliest bits of myself and back into the streets that teemed with all signs of life. Beyond perceptions of good versus bad lies an altogether different form of power.

In this universe, there are no harbingers on the horizon, only happenings that flower from collaborative forces: The future is made from the macro movements of the cosmos, our micro maneuvers down on the ground, and everything in between, all firing together in this very moment. Free from the constraints of blame-based causality, we are free to take up all of our life's causes—suspending our judgment, befriending what's meeting us, sensing how it wants to move, and helping it move along.

This is the discovery of soul purpose: the marriage of our personal will with the will of this whole wild world.

Charting Your Course

For most of us, our first formal encounter with astrology is through the broad strokes of our Sun sign (also known as our "zodiac sign" or "star sign") and then through the more personalized lens of our astrological birth chart.

A blueprint of the cosmos that shows the arrangement of the celestial bodies at the moment we debuted, our **birth chart** reveals our creative challenges and calls to action in this incarnation (fig I.1). At the heart of this chart sits our **Sun sign**, which marks us with a singular mission: We are here to take up its cause and let its energy course through us. Behind the Sun's glisten of exposure sits our **Moon sign**, a more nocturnal shade of self that imbues us with emotional atmosphere and unconscious nature. And to alchemize the two, we have our **Rising sign**. The sign that was emerging on the eastern horizon when we materialized, our Rising sign is the front door through which we meet life and self—a thematic refrain that leads us on the adventure of our lifetime. Together, these three pieces form our dynamic core: a mission, a mood, and a destined meeting.

From here, each of us has a whole suite of planets placed in different signs (that is, our Sun sign might be Capricorn while our Venus sign might be Aquarius). We each have different sign saturation points. For example, we may have planets placed in Virgo, but none in Scorpio. When three or more planets sit within a single sign, we've got a **stellium**—an amplification of energy that invites us to become extra intimate with that sign archetype.

You could spend lifetimes trying to untangle the chart's lines and interpret its calculations. And while there is value to the specificity of astrology's machinations, some of this technical tangle is also evidence of how the art's inherently intuitive qualities have been co-opted by our cultural obsession with the codifiable, provable, rational, and, in fact, chart-able. In my perusal of *Parkers'* I skipped right over the pages on how to compute this tangle using calculators and protractors—instructions hidden all the way in the back and definitely not printed in full color or high gloss. My eleven-year-old self was already too busy exploring the zodiac out in the wild, as some-

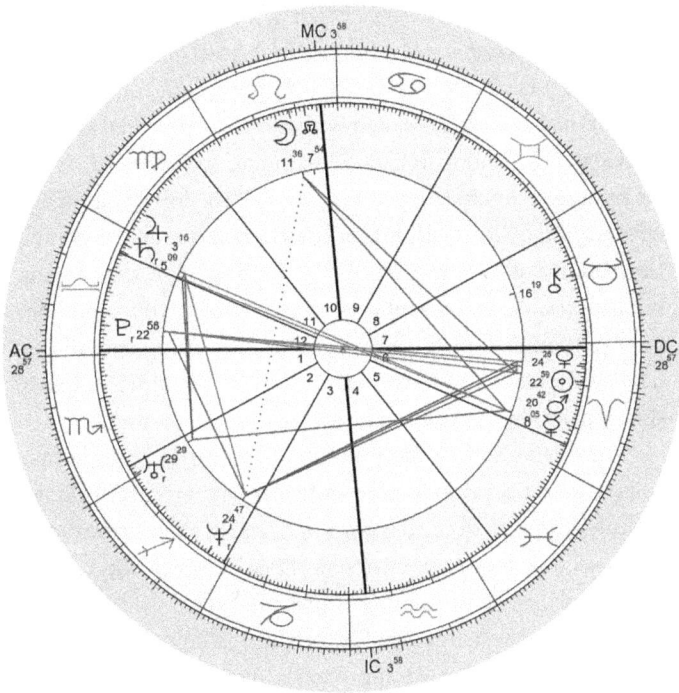

I.1 A map of the cosmos at the time of our birth, the astrological birth chart divides the sky into twelve sections. Beginning with the Rising sign, labeled as AC or ascendent, and moving counterclockwise, we see an outer wheel of twelve zodiac signs. Next is an inner wheel of celestial bodies that sit within those signs, separated into pie pieces, called houses. The lines of communication that run between parts of the chart are called aspects. The Sun sign is the doughnut with the dot in the center of the circle, and the Moon sign is the crescent slice. Chart image generated by astro.com.

thing breathable and wearable that sprang from the dynamic experience of the world rather than a representation of it.

Star Charting is not a book about how to explain every cranny of your birth chart, cast your horoscope, or crack the code of the cosmos. Instead, it is a practice of personal and collective poetics and a process of reanimating the world. When we practice star charting, we begin with the inhabitation and observation of life itself, rather than letting our charts delimit the cadence of our experience. You both *are* and *are not* your birth chart. As you travel through this book, you will honor your personal zodiacal saturation points. And you will also head "off-road" and beyond the chart to encounter signs of the signs wherever you roam.

The **twelve zodiac signs** illuminate a journey of the human spirit through a rainbow of evolutionary experience. This adventure begins with the first sign of Aries, in all its va-va-voom verbness. And it ends in the ethers of Pisces, which Slip 'n Slides us beyond our stable notions of self.

These are twelve modes of perceiving, listening to, and bearing witness to life. Twelve approaches to meeting it and moving with its currents. Twelve ways of not losing heart. And twelve styles of co-creating change that are born from channeling the power that moves through all of us—and through everything else with a beat.

Tracing this arc, *Star Charting* invites you to rock and roll through the natural rhythms of all of life. Each year, the Sun spends about a month in each sign: The year starts in Aries season with the spring or fall equinox (depending on your hemisphere) in late March, and ends in Pisces season, twelve months later on the other side. During each of these **sign seasons**, life on the ground dialogues with that archetype and invites all of us — regardless of our personal chart — into communion with its themes.

Each of these twelve signs is made from one of the **four elements**: the stuff that already surrounds you and lives within you, present in everything from a burner flame to a bubble bath. Fire gives us life force. Earth gives us form. Air gives us freedom. And water gives us back.

Each of these elements is then filtered through one of the **three modalities**: cardinal, fixed, and mutable (there are cardinal, fixed, and mutable fire signs, and so on through the elements). We arise through the four cardinal signs that initiate each season; we abide in the fixed signs that steady each season's center; and we disseminate in the mutable signs, where the season falls away.

Within each chapter, you'll encounter a sign's energy through a **quartet of practices**. Because this book is born from the belief that the practice of star charting is synonymous with the practice of living — that astrology *is* life — I'll first bring it alive the only way I can: through my own existence. Next, I'll invite you to witness it from a greater distance. Then, you'll make it a part of your story. And finally, we'll free it together.

Throughout all of these practices, we will approach the signs as living entities that are present within each of us, and within all of life, in different concentrations at different moments. The signs are this book's truest protagonists: They are the spirits seeking to express themselves through our flesh. They are what give us animation. And as we channel them consciously, we give them, and all of life in turn, more spirit.

The words written in this book are intended as more than just conveyors of meaning. The poetics are part of the sensory practice of bringing the signs into being—spoken as a kind of full-bodied onomatopoeia where the sounds of the sign sound like the sign itself. This is language as incantation and invocation. As part of your star charting practice, feel free to cast spells: Read passages aloud without grasping for analytical meaning and see what is summoned.

While each sign has a core form and feeling tone, there are infinite interpretative variations and no right or wrong resonances. I encourage you to take these energies and make them your own by developing new associations and speaking astrology in an accent that is yours alone. One way to do so is to start by identifying a "magic key" for each sign that is highly personal: a scent, scene, sound, sensation that immediately opens you into its lifeworld. An inherited fur coat might be your gateway to Capricorn's timeless majesty. A tube of suntan lotion might unveil Leo's emblazoned heart.

As you follow these interconnected registers and rhythms of our practice, a biodiverse symphony of being will begin to build inside of you and around you: colliding, beholding, channeling, and divining.

Colliding

We each meet our self by meeting life according to our own matter and alchemizing it into something more. Each sign chapter in this book opens with my own personal practice of astrology: close encounters with the signs that have composed my life. They are inevitably infused with the scorched, splashy style that's emblematic of my Aries-Leo-Mars-Pluto–heavy makeup. The signs have been served to me in unsubtle forms, Minute Maid frozen juice concentrate style. And I have often met my self through fighting, fucking, and life-forcing in the face of death.

Throughout these stories, many practices proliferate—lipsticking, flying, feasting, strutting—evidence that when imbued with attention and meaning, all forms of living are always already forms of divining. Beyond all the glitter and grit of these tales, the heart that beats at the center conveys the omnipresence of spirit in its rollicking range of forms and the possibility of encountering divinity at any depth. And beyond their particularity to me, these bits of memoir still carry the universal, archetypal shape of their elements. My fire-sign stories spark my own self at their center. The earth chapters are weightier and more finite, charting my body and time. My air missives trend to the abstract and speak of translations. Water tales dance with returns, releases, and endings.

They are the love poems of an astrology that's made from encounter and exchange. While my fiery self flames throughout, these stories share my lifelong practice of harnessing the signs to become new rhinestone-stick-on sides of self and to go elsewhere. When we meet the signs on their terms and give more of ourselves to them, they give themselves right back. As I lived these stories, and processed them through writing, I had to face Aries, earn Capricorn, let Gemini elude me, and feel Taurus delight me.

Meeting the signs means exploring the tension between our willingness to morph and our deep knowledge of what is immutable within us. We unlock the doors to the divine by fitting ourselves to the keyholes without losing our original form.

Beholding

In the second part of each chapter, we'll embrace a sensation-based practice of coming alive to the sign's presence. Here, the sign is introduced as a current of energy that flows through all of life. For example, the Cancer archetype, rather than taking the form of a cookie-baking caretaker that we either "are" or "are not," becomes a current of homing, encircling, and gestating—evident in everything from the evening rush of workers heading back to their lairs to the cycles of the almighty tides. Through this part of our practice, you'll be invited to simply notice the energy in the world around you and within you, and to hold it in beauty and power without having to understand or analyze it.

Channeling

After beholding in beauty, we'll engage in a personal-inquiry practice of bringing the sign into self-awareness. Here, you'll seek signals of this sign within yourself and your life in order to better understand how it flows through you and only you. Through this section of our practice, you'll explore your personal inflection points: noticing whether or not you have any planets placed in a particular sign and what relationship you have with the sign's qualities. We honor what's here, and we become curious about what's less present. Because in a cosmos of inherent aliveness, nothing is ever truly gone.

Whether or not you're packing planets in a sign, you'll also be invited to find more ways of accessing each through its **ruling celestial body**. For example, while we might not all have planets placed in the freewheeling sign of Sagittarius in our birth chart, each of us has a Jupiter sign (Sag's ruling planet) in our chart that encourages us to build more faith.

Rather than memorizing a cookbook of astrological interpretation (à la What does it mean if I have Jupiter in Libra?), you'll be invited to explore your placements through an elements-based practice of energy awareness (for example, Libra is an air sign, so what might it feel like to access the faith that Jupiter promises through the expansive possibilities of air?). I'll provide you with a way to start playing that's inspired by my own associations (for example, for me the vigor of the planet Mars comes alive as our astrological "blood type"), and I encourage you to use this as a launchpad into making your own metaphors and meaning. You can find your planets on a free site like astro.com or cafeastrology.com, or simply by internet searches like "What's my Venus sign?" If you're more advanced, you can play with layering these practices and incorporating houses, aspects, and transits.

Additionally, each of the **tarot's twenty-two Major Arcana cards** is imbued with a concentrated form of astrological essence. This resonance between the cards and the cosmos stems from the same archetypal innateness that informs all of astrology. For example, Sagittarius's sprawling wildfire current already courses throughout life, and the Wheel of Fortune and Temperance cards are two places where it happens to spring to the surface to be felt and seen. Tarot is deeply embedded in my astrological practice, and I find that working with the cards brings the zodiac symbols into accessible and vivid Technicolor by revealing new tones in their palettes. It also reminds me of the intuitive, emergent quality of astrology. Just like we might flip a tarot card to see what's "revealed," we can see what signs and planets sparkle for us in a given moment and follow their guidance, rather than delimiting our experience of divinity through birth-chart dogma.

You can choose to work with each sign's tarot cards in an intentional way, perhaps by taking them out of the deck and magnetizing them to your kitchen fridge or propping them up on a dashboard as you travel through a chapter's practices. You can also use them in a divination-based way by isolating these twenty-two cards, drawing one "blind" from the pack, and letting it guide you to work with a particular sign (say, if you pluck the Fool card from the pack, you could dive deeper into the Aquarius chapter). And don't worry if you don't have a tarot deck; you can always just write down the names of the twenty-two cards on the backs of uniform index cards.

Divining

Finally, we'll place these sign currents within the larger context of a co-creative universe and explore how we can harness them to effect collective change. You can call on the credos in this section as a kind of magical manifesto that can spark broader conversations in your community.

You're encouraged to gather with a partner, a group of colleagues, family members, other beloveds, or strangers to embrace these cosmic commitments—either during that sign's particular season or at any time when its principles could benefit your sense of interconnection and future possibility. While we all certainly have access to each sign's energies regardless of our personal astrology, cultivating a biodiversity of shared beingness can also happen by calling upon our sign "specialists." People with particular sign placements—especially the

Sun, Moon, and Rising—can become our beacons who uphold these qualities and help show us their way.

Your Path Through the Practices

Each of us is here to have at the whole of the zodiac on our terms, and I encourage you to divine your own path through the practices. If you're brand-new, you might start by reading about your Sun sign and build from there, perhaps next looking to your Moon and Rising signs. Together, your **Sun/Moon/ Rising** signs form the trinity of you, and their qualities exist in rhythmic exchange. We stretch toward the individuated exposure of our Sun, we shelter into our Moon's shade, and we greet our Rising's adventurous invitation. You can sample these signs singularly as you need them and also start to explore their alchemical intersections.

Beyond your birth chart, you can also apply the **astrological energies as elixirs**: choosing to select a sign chapter that you feel could best support you during a certain life moment. You can do this consciously. Or you can do it unconsciously by closing your eyes and flipping to a section of the book or by isolating those twenty-two tarot cards and pulling one to lead you to the corresponding sign's chapter.

Finally, above all, you can chart your course from **Aries to Pisces as a complete soul program**. You might experience this like an exploratory yearbook, where you follow along month-by-month from Aries season in late March all the way to Pisces season on the other side. But there's no need to confine yourself to strict seasonal dates. You can always seek the solar power of Leo energy in the depths of a Capricornian winter, or explore the distinction between Libra's autumnal clarity and Scorpio's fall composting. This archetypal adventure can be tapped over any measure of time—over the course of twelve weeks, twelve days, twelve hours, or twelve minutes—where the chapters offer twelve ways of being in, and with, this wild world.

Astrology asks us to behold ourselves in all of our multitudes. It is a practice of coming closer, coming together, and putting our hands on all parts of this planet—even, and especially, the parts we'd rather keep at bay. When we star chart, we befriend both the familiar and the strange and cease to be strangers. We turn against separateness in all directions and say: *I am another you and you and you, too*. And god is everywhere.

Aries

Vivifying + Vitalizing

In my origin story, I came from nothing but Aries. It was the sinew so synonymous with my self that I couldn't see any part of it as other. I felt it in the forward lean of my bony little body on the playground, guarding the pinprick bugs from execution by magnifying-glass flame and CPR-ing the stomped springtime worms. Everything that was alive had to keep on living. And as long as I stayed upright and ready to back it by doing battle, I'd make sure that not a single blade of grass got left behind.

I tasted it in the Olympic dreams of gold glory that animated every push of my person against the elements and into the world. In races through the neighborhood on my scooter, emblazoned with one word — *Challenger* — faster and faster in the fierce face of the wind. Denting the turquoise chlorine from the high dive with a flash of hot pink Lisa Frank leopard swimsuit. Cocksure choreography to thumping hothouse beats in the basement. *This is the rhythm of my life.* Agitating the particles of air with the punch of my limbs, I was here to have at it, and "against" was my emblem of aliveness.

I heard it in the rush outside my bedroom window at dusk, as the mojo machines moved northbound along I-95, bound for bigger cities where the adult me was distilled into a singular, prophetic vision: I saw my grown-up body standing straight before a midnight panorama with a rocks glass in my hand and a rotating cast of shadowy lovers behind me. Sent to sleep against my will, I'd dream a recurring dream where a crowd of taunters scoffed: "You won't jump. You can't do it." And then, of course, I did: I pounced from a dizzying ledge all the way down to the ground.

When the neighborhood kids and I played house, I'd drag my stuffed animals into the closet to keep up the charade of motherhood. But I'd be the single mom in a studio apartment, recording my one-woman radio show on the handheld tape recorder I'd hold to my chest like a badge of honor. A part of everything that had anima because I demanded to remain forever apart, I showed up to second grade one morning and became myself: Declaring my name was now "Bess," I refused to answer to any other, as I pressed the letters of my chosen title into the paper so hard that they turned to braille.

Then, at age thirteen, propped against the bathroom sink of the Seahorse Motel on the South Jersey shore, I learned to put Aries on straight. Leaning my life toward the mirror with a steady hand, I twisted the white plastic tube until the tip of Wet *n* Wild's crushed-velvet stick licked my lips.

As I hit the boardwalk each night, I built my body from scratch. My footsteps became a full-on strut. Each movement I made, made me. Instead of Venus on the half shell, I was Mars in a muscle car motored by my own mettle. Mothers clutched young boys to their chests as I passed, hissing: *Never date girls who wear lipstick like that*.

I dare you, I spoke back.

Defiance was destiny.

Every day from that day forward, I'd put it on to turn it on. Wet *n* Wild graduated to Cover Girl Cranberry and Revlon Cherries in the Snow. Whether squid ink, Barbie pink, or watermelon ball, the punch of the pigment remained the same.

With each application, Aries created the world from scratch. As I held my dynamite stick steady, all the burning women in my family line were blown to dust and I appeared out of nothing at all, alone and upright in the daring dirt. Here, Aries' impulse existed without any reference point. Lipsticking was objectless in its all-consuming aim, the ignition switch to a self where nothing stood outside of it.

In the beginning, there was only this: With the tip of Aries against my lips, my life was all mine.

Beholding Aries: Turning It On

The Aries current is already alive and well within you and all around you. To spark it, you can begin by noticing *how things come to life*, unstoppably and irrepressibly. The first streaks of sunrise. The laughter that effervesces out of a loved one's lips. A dog let out the back door with a case of the canine "zoomies."

The microgreen mojo of a tiny shoot flexing its way up through the pavement cracks.

Before you work your will, take a moment to let the Aries current do its work on you:

As you wake in the morning, begin by simply starting up your body. Send the force of life into each limb and "turn on" the switch in each sinew. Separate yourself from sleep. You are not the ether of your dreams any longer. You have peeled off the strip of night and you are upright.

Don't linger in your pajamas or wait to wash your face. Stare straight into the mirror and say your name aloud. Look around you and call things by their most minimalistic epithets, as if you were learning their language for the very first time. Hard. Soft. Want. Don't Want. To Do. Done.

Charge yourself with straightforward foods snagged fresh and ready. A hunk of direct-from-the-farm mozzarella. A perfectly crisp apple. A torn scrap of newly baked bread. No fancy swirls in your cappuccino or fifteen-ingredient smoothies. Just uncomplicated fuel for the force that is you.

Notice how life doesn't actually need all that much to get up and get going.

Zip into your equivalent of a bodysuit—clothing with no fuss that allows you to remain aerodynamic and unencumbered. Get ready to go from day to night without having to add or subtract anything. Fit for whatever, whenever, however. No extra changes of shoes. No dressing up or dressing down. Whatever you sport, stick with it from dawn to dusk.

Channeling Aries: You're Here

Aries marks the very first spot on our zodiacal journey. Never before and never again will we stand here, entirely alone, with nothing to lose and everything to give. Rugged and nonreferential, Aries' imperative to exist emerges from the primordial ooze of the twelfth sign of Pisces, and it sloughs off Pisces' selflessness to come clean through the singularity of self.

Aries is **Cardinal Fire**. The initiation and instigation of the fire element, this sign's core call is sheer here-ness. Because we cannot argue with our animation, our existence cannot be an accident. And the force of this existence is a fact: Even if we "do nothing" we are still here, displacing particles of air. Aries reminds us that life is going to go on, with or without us. So we may as well put our backs into it and rally to take up all of creation's cause.

As you uncover Aries in your own birth chart, you can begin with its sign symbol, which sits at the start of this chapter, also known as the **Aries glyph**. There is an inevitability to tracing this form along its straight spine. A leanness to its libido. It bursts into being from base to font. And it penetrates a single point back down from font to base. In its stark simplicity, form and function fuse as one. Experiment with sketching a version of your own—this is astrology as both referential alphabet and improvisational inhabitation.

Alive in this symbol, you can then feel for the presence or absence of **Aries planets in your birth chart**. Notice both the on switches where Aries planets exist and the dormant spots that await provocation through Aries' push.

From here, fan out into Aries' facets by exploring its family of associated planets and cards.

Mars: Your Life Blood

Aries' ruling planet, Mars, is the pulse of life: the innate blood flow that imbues everything that's alive with its own beat. Through it, we press the world with our thumbprints and see the irrefutable effects of our existence dented on the planet's surface. *I am here. I was here.*

Mars is the engine that makes things happen and gets things done on a personal plane. But at its core, no matter what it's doing or not doing, it is our drumbeat in the face of death. It will live for as long as we do. And it is the energy that brings us back to life. When we are bottomed out or bereft, Mars turns on and steps forward to keep us alive. It's a champion of our original cause to have been created in the first place.

In astrology, Mars operates as the arm of the Sun. If our Sun (which we'll meet in the second fire sign, Leo) is our made-for-only-us mission of a lifetime, Mars is the mojo that keeps our blood pumping while we make good on it.

To come alive to Mars's properties, you can start by asking yourself:

What turns me on? What brings me upright? What is my energetic constitution? How does life flow through me?

We've all got the planet Mars placed in a particular sign in our birth chart. Locate your own Mars sign, feel for the animation of its element (Mars in Fire, Earth, Air, or Water), and ask yourself:

What would it feel like to fuel myself through this sign and its element? How can I trust that it is actively advocating to keep me alive in every moment, no matter what moves I make?

You can use these blood types for inspiration:

Mars in Fire (Aries/Leo/Sagittarius) *Carnivores*. Fueling your force through direct impact and expressing vitality by celebrating whatever has lifeblood flowing through it.

Earth (Taurus/Virgo/Capricorn) *Herbivores*. Fueling your force through sustainable effort and expressing vitality by honoring the specific purpose of each entity that already exists.

Air (Gemini/Libra/Aquarius) *Omnivores*. Fueling your force through connections and expressing vitality by letting even inanimate concepts carry a charge that can charge you.

Water (Cancer/Scorpio/Pisces) *Pescatarians*. Fueling your force through hidden reserves and expressing vitality by both magnetizing and being magnetized as the mood strikes you.

The Emperor and the Tower: The Forces Are With You

Each of the tarot's twenty-two Major Arcana cards is infused with a zodiacal essence, and we can summon the cards to reveal new tones in each sign's palette. The Aries cards are direct and daring invitations to animate. In the **Emperor**, we come alive to the fact and force of our own existence: the mark we make and the effect of our hereness. And in the **Tower**, we come alive to the fact of every force that surrounds us — ending subject-driven strategy about who's doing what to whom and getting ready to move as the moment demands — for, against, with, or any which way in between.

When exploring the Emperor, ask yourself:

What is my impact? How can I lay claim to both my right to exist and the responsibility for my existence?

What stance am I being asked to take? Is it a moment for amplifying my footprint? Or for relaxing excessive efforts to prove I'm still here?

When exploring the Tower, ask yourself:

Which forces in my life feel like they're "for" me? Which feel like they're "against" me? Which feel like they're "with" me?

When I release a little bit of attachment to my personal will, what unstoppable energy wants to be unleashed? What can I no longer hold back?

Divining Aries: The Art of Emerging

In a world before the arrival of elevated Aries energy, we "just do it" only to prove it. Phallic power becomes penetrative, extractive, and purely egoistic. We barrel through barriers out of fear of growing flaccid instead of from our joy of bringing alive.

At one extreme, Aries energy morphs into an oversized adolescent who shock-jocks life just to get a rise. And at the other end of the spectrum, with a complete lack of Aries, we flounder, forceless and faceless, shrinking from the spark of self and refusing to make anything at all out of our one-shot existence.

When wielded consciously, Aries' greatest gift is **the art of emerging**. Here, we give up our obsession with who's doing what to whom and ask: What needs to be done here? We are firm in the fact of our existence without needing to flex it; we listen for the invitations to action instead of aggressing only our agenda; and we take up the causes that fuse with the most necessary verbs of the world. Experienced in this way, Aries becomes a brave balm of being and doing acting as one. The singular actor and the seamless action collapse, and each and every thing that makes a move makes life happen, all together.

An Aries future asks us to embrace virility, viridity, and friction.

Virility

We celebrate the pulse of every being on this planet by recognizing its right to exist, the potential of its potency, and the distinctive mark that it leaves as it moves through the world. We broaden the definitions of virility and libido beyond gender and sexuality to honor all forms of heat, uprightness, and animation. We expand our understanding of how things get done and who is doing them by interrogating the binaries of perpetrator versus victim, subject versus object, and doing versus non-doing. We commit to exalting all the forces that exist on all scales.

Viridity

We embrace greenness: the moment-by-moments, come-from-nothings, and start-from-scratches. We allow space for strategy-less, nonreferential actions to arise without having to explain their origins. We let each other operate leanly and cleanly. We don't owe anyone anything or have anything to prove. We support each other's birthright to be here as reason enough to take an action. And we acknowledge that we have never been *right here* ever before; no matter how long we've existed or how much we've seen, we always have the chance to birth the world anew. We commit to showing up with a freshness of spirit and to having a shot at life, again and again.

Friction

We commit to exploring our aliveness even when it feels confronting to do so. We learn to distinguish between unnecessary aggression versus necessary provocation and evolutionary friction. We interrogate the roots of our rage and purify this force so that it can support expressive creation. We become the protagonists of our own lives by first standing *apart*: evidencing our separateness and granting others the right to stand at the center of their own existence. From this place as protagonists, we harness our individuation to send heat toward heroics. We stand *for* what needs championing and protecting. We stand *against* what demands dismantling. And we move *with* what must be moved.

2   **Taurus**

Absorbing + Retaining

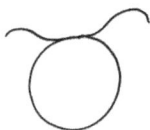

I found Taurus packed inside Mom Mom's kitchen cabinets. Bulk bags of Kraft caramel squares that coated your mouth like a cave of sweetness. Chalky pastel Smarties popped like over-the-counter pills. Snack packs of Bar-B-Q Fritos I'd let rest on my tongue until the smoke became honey.

Inside the freezer, the feast was even more florid. An accumulation of boxed cakes, stacked single-serving Ellio's pizzas, and buckets of ice-cream bonbons with the thin chocolate coating that'd turn to vanilla against a tap from your teeth. All the neighborhood kids would come clamoring for a glimpse inside the infamous treasure chest that satisfied every kind of Willy Wonka craving.

There was always more than enough.

This feast had flowered from fallow ground. On a crooked Memphis porch as a child, Mom Mom's luckiest Christmas brought a single gift of a round, ripe orange. And now, all the way up here on the Eastern Seaboard, she had a whole bowl of nuts to crack open. An always filled-to-the-brim tumbler of whiskey and Coke. A Newport to leisurely drag on from the hollow of her hand.

The family philosophy followed her lead to "live it up," said with an upward flick of the wrist. I brought my lunch money to the family poker table and took my chances, betting all-or-nothing against the specter of that other life of lack. On a dinner out, the hungry ghost still lived in Mom Mom's stomach. She'd wrap our uneaten rolls in tissues, hide whole desserts in her hat, and slip shiny packets of butter into her purse like golden tickets. To have and to hold. Hers at long last.

She birthed seven babies, and the first four were all earth signs, three Tauruses among them. The eldest, my Taurus Sun sign mother, developed the habit of holding food in her cheeks as a child. At nighttime teeth cleaning, Mom Mom would pry her clenched jaw open and discover the storehouse of soft food inside. My mother's closed mouth was a memory—an animal in amber sent from a Southern season where sweetness had once been scarce. When she was nearly the age her mother had been when she died, I watched my nearly gone Taurus mother be resurrected from her ICU bed with only one thing to say: *I'm hungry.*

My body was next in line to receive a different kind of bounty. At seventeen, unleashed on the city of Rome, alone, I spread those stolen butter packets through the streets, reveling in the feast my Roman Catholic family had ferreted away. *Arrabiata*, *carbonara*, *gricia*. Coconut ice cream scraped out of tawny shells and sheets of pink prosciutto peeled off the plate. In the shuttered room where I slept, the sweltering temperatures brought the air to a full stop. Laid out on the sheets like an offering to the pagan gods, I cooked in my own juices.

And everywhere and anywhere, I made love. With strangers more than double my age met in laundromats where I spun my sweat-drenched skirts, and outside gelaterias where I licked my stracciatella with a lush tongue. My body bloomed and I splayed my petals against the crumbling walls in full view of the Vatican. Fed through my Aries fire, this Taurus form of flowering burned the bounty into ever more fuel for my life force. I was La Lupa, dripping the fat, salt, and sugar to the suckling Romulus and Remus beneath. And I was those babies, lapping it up in the name of a new land.

This was the promiscuous plenty of Taurus, made possible only by generations who had wrapped the dinner rolls and buried them deep in the bottom of a hard-earned handbag like tubers planted for another time. Because of all that, there was all this: my Taurus-ruled Empress tarot card on ecstasy, where I could become both stamen and pistil. Fully self-pollinating, I took my pleasure.

The weekend before my father took his life, he confessed the saddest center of his story to my mother. As a child, he'd been left entirely alone. His father, deep in the Thermos factory. His mother shuttered up at the farm, fingers forming hair rollers on the family assembly line. Gone hungry at dinnertime, he'd hunt: soundlessly appearing outside the kitchen windows of neighbors to witness the warmth of their suppers. High-shine chicken thighs spread-eagled across plastic-fruit-printed tablecloths. Serving spoons plunged into pureed potatoes. But he couldn't ask to sit down and be served. He'd starve from the shame instead. Or disappear into the woods behind the tight little houses to siphon off some sustenance from whatever animal or vegetable could be found.

After his death, I found his last supper stored in Mom Mom's fridge. Mountains of Mediterranean mezze, stacked carefully, bearing the marks of where his hands and mouth had been. Final dips into hummus wet sand, a deep valley he'd traveled through rough red muhammara. A Hansel-and-Gretel trail of pistachio shells on the parquet. Out in the shed, we'd find the stacks of cash he'd hidden. Elsewhere, it was held in faraway accounts under assumed names. As a boy, he'd dreamed of buried treasure beneath all this dirt. A lockbox of liquid gold without limit.

In my birth chart, the lone placement in Taurus is the planetoid Chiron. The tenderest, touchiest spot in our chart, Chiron tells a tale of a hurt in our heart that can't be healed. An inherited absence beyond the explicable and the fixable, which asks only for the fullness of presence. The ability to hallow our hunger.

In Mom Mom's kitchen, my father's trail of pistachio shells caught at the soles of my feet for weeks. Each one was a hollow that I was here to hold.

Beholding Taurus: Filling Up

To touch Taurus's current, you can start by noticing *how things flower into fullness and take their fill.* A tank at a gas pump topped to the brim. A soft-serve ice-cream cone swirled to the edges. A ripe scent giving off its goodness. Observe how so much of what surrounds you fulfills itself by first leaning back and taking up life like a buttercup. And see how this process of growing laden becomes its own form of sensual strength—the courage to have it and hold it for as long as it's here.

Next, let the Taurus current do its work on you:

As you wake, begin with as much ampleness as possible. Consider what you could first take up tangibly from your environment, before you lean forward into the tasks ahead. Languidly stretch with limbs spread. Sink securely into the divot your body makes as it presses against the mattress. Let the daybreak flood your form and luxuriate in the light, allowing it to coax you from the sheets. Take your pleasure from it, and give it yours in kind.

Before you even reach the kitchen, start deriving sustenance from the scents, sounds, and sights that fill your rooms. When you make it to the actual food sources, consider what would feel most delectable and five-sensual, regardless of nutritional standards. Maybe you eat an ice cream sandwich to start your day. Or maybe it's muesli. No matter.

Slip into something more comfortable than you'd usually choose. Material that touches you back and gives you room to sense your own movements—like feeling the pleat of a loose pant billowing back against your body after you take a step. Pick fragrances you want to keep smelling on your own skin all day, then anoint yourself and sniff them. Become redolent and receive your scent in return.

Channeling Taurus: Receiving Your Richness

Taurus is the second spot on the zodiacal wheel. In Aries, we experience emergence: bursting into never-before-seen life. Then, in Taurus, we experience inherence: learning to live better by lapping up what we've already got.

Taurus is **Fixed Earth.** Fixed energy relishes the essence of its element in a self-replenishing state. It is the core power that sits at the center of each season. In our first expression of it, in our first florescence of the earth element, we deepen our deposits and strengthen our reserves. Taurus's earthly riches are full and dense, hanging low and heavy like ripe fruit.

Begin with the **Taurus glyph.** Notice the dinner-plate thickness of this symbol, with two handles at the top to hold the curvaceous serving platter. An unbroken rounded edge that retains the richness. Licked clean in the center and awaiting another helping.

Once you are secure in this symbol, you can then feel for the presence or absence of **Taurus planets in your birth chart.** Notice both the flush houses where these planets flower and the places devoid of them that await infill.

From here, fan out into Taurus's facets by exploring its family of associated planets and cards.

Venus: Your Scent

Taurus's ruling planet, Venus, is the emission of life's natural fragrance. We are lured by its scent and we allure life through it, attracting more of what we adore by giving off its essence.

While Mars is all make-it-happen mojo, Venus is mutual magnetics. As we open to let in our love of life, it opens in turn, and we partake in the shared dilation of desire. We each have our own form of effusion and reception. Some of us emit subtle, close-to-the-skin scents and are carefully coaxed toward opening. Others have a musky silage that can be tracked for miles and can turn on the flood of honey with one love tap.

Start by asking yourself:

What am I drawn to and how do I draw it toward me? What do I enjoy? What enjoys me?

Then, you can dive deeper and explore your own Venus sign. Settle into the richness of your Venus sign and its element and ask yourself:

How does this sign and its element take its pleasure and taste this world? What would it feel like to both give off and get back from it?

You can use these scents for inspiration:

Venus in Fire (Aries/Leo/Sagittarius) *Body Spray*. Dilating to what delivers frankness and forthrightness, and receiving pleasure by trusting in honesty and heroism.

Earth (Taurus/Virgo/Capricorn) *Essential Oil*. Dilating to what delivers direct support and solid value, and receiving pleasure by trusting in self-replenishing cycles of empty and full.

Air (Gemini/Libra/Aquarius) *Incense Stick*. Dilating to what delivers curiosity and illumination, and receiving pleasure by trusting in what passes through life's swinging doors.

Water (Cancer/Scorpio/Pisces) *Shea Butter*. Dilating to what delivers intimacy and fusion, and receiving pleasure by trusting in enchantment and immersive experience.

The Empress and the Hierophant:
You Are What You Eat

These Taurus cards are rich repositories of receipt and retention. The **Empress** is our mystical maximalist: it absorbs life's inherent cornucopia and helps us convert any sensation into flower food. Meanwhile, the **Hierophant** stores our accumulated resources: it asks us to make good use of the muscle memories we've already earned through experience and to interrogate when entrenched patterns might be keeping us stuck.

When exploring the Empress, ask yourself:

How do I receive from the world—compliments, sensory pleasure, physical touch, resources? Where would I like to open further and how could I support this dilation?

What is my relationship with moments of "moreness"— saturated sensation, effluence, or profusion? No matter my situation, what more does this very moment want to give me, and how can I partake of its fullest flavor?

When exploring the Hierophant, ask yourself:

What do I hold within me? How do I retain resources, and what beliefs and experiences are stored deep in my bones?

What's familiar to me? Are there resources and wisdom I've already acquired that I can apply here? And where might I be functioning from a place of overfamiliarity—expecting to encounter more of the same and reacting from past patterning rather than in present tense?

Divining Taurus: The Art of Replenishing

In a world before the arrival of elevated Taurus energy, we hunger for what we don't have, and we hoard what we already hold. Our distribution of richness becomes violently uneven, and moreness means only material acquisition, stripped of all magic.

At one extreme, Taurus energy swallows the storehouse whole and gets stuck in the honey pot, obsessed with guarding its goods. And at the other end of the spectrum, with a lack of any Taurus, we're left bereft of life's butter: shut down to our senses because of our belief that sweetness is only superficial or that we don't really merit a full meal anyway.

When wielded consciously, Taurus's greatest gift is **the art of replenishing**. In this state, we are naturally replete with resources and are able to abide the self-restocking cycles of empty and full. From this rooted place, we grasp the true promise of Taurus's promiscuity: the plenitude of being alive in a body and allowing our form to become flush with all the stuff of life. Experienced in this way, Taurus becomes a balm of bounty that drinks down to the last drop without anticipating any hunger ahead.

A Taurus future asks us to embrace plenty, satisfaction, and ease.

Plenty

Without damaging our nervous systems or breaking necessary boundaries, we become ample with the inherent richness of living in a sensual world in sensate bodies. We honor the particularity of how, what, and how much we are each available to take in from life. And we challenge the limits placed on our sensuality that spring from scarcity, unworthiness, and shame around "too muchness." We encourage each other to become more omnivorous by expanding our preferences and restrictive definitions of good/bad pleasures, exploring how we can convert any matter that meets us into more food for our bodies and spirits.

Satisfaction

We commit to understanding when enough is enough: materially, emotionally, spiritually. We attend to our hungry ghosts and acquisitive anxieties so that we don't bring our starving hearts to others' tables. We learn to enjoy what we've already got, and we learn to long for what we don't have in ways that give us more life rather than take away from it. Together, we face the very real fact of unequal distribution of resources by cultivating equitable energetic exchange. We discover what helps us feel resourced enough to give away a surplus when there is one. We learn how to ask for what we need when there's lack and identify the sources that best sustain us through changing seasons. In any circumstance, we ask ourselves honestly: What have I got to give? And what do I need to receive?

Ease

We commit to dismantling the belief system that *hard* always equals *better* and that pleasure must always be earned. We look at where we make things unnecessarily difficult for ourselves and each other. We seek more available relaxation in forms that are not strictly based on reward for effort. We invite one another to become indigenous within our own lives by honoring each person's inherent knowledge and earned experiential resources and by creating conditions that increase our comfort, no matter the context. We settle in together and let more of life come to us, instead of always contorting ourselves to match our surroundings.

Gemini

Channeling + Conveying

In my boxy slippers and mint chiffon, I followed Gemini's flicker across the floor, summoned by the spirits inside Mrs. Emory's upright piano. As the Russian ballet mistress's wooden stick went down, down, down, we'd go up, up, up. Lifting. Lighter. Levitating.

On the threshold between childhood and some other age, the doctors told me my bones were growing all wrong. A jutting jaw might just have to be wired shut, resigning me to muteness and milkshakes. A spine had taken a sharp turn and could be forced into a sticky papier-mâché chrysalis until it found the one right way forward.

But beneath the threat of casts and wires, my bones were still breathing. And I was becoming other. The ballerinas before me multiplied the color wheel of middle school metamorphosis. Would I become Marina Castagna, with her bubble-letter heart face, effervescent from the inside like she'd swallowed an

Alka-Seltzer secret in one bite? Or Amber Wolf, always late, often gone, and the best one out of us all—a glitter stud in the side of her nose and a body so ruthless she could ride it however she wanted. And Melinda Reed forever. With her plush peach lips that needed no stick, whispering conspiratorially behind a half-open palm. Her sushi-thin skin tugged taut against her leotard, washed so many times you could see the green felt curling into fronds. Behind her at the barre, while we worked our bodies into the same shape over and over to turn them different, she was almost close enough to pet.

I found the magazine headline at the newsstand, squeezed between *Baby-Sitters Club Spring Break Super Specials* and *Betty & Veronica Double Digests*. I poured the coins onto the counter and raced home on slippered feet to slide it beneath a stack of prized covers featuring the Gemini Sun Angelina Jolie—a brand-new star with bleached, buzzed hair and sleeves rolled like a mechanic, revealing inky dragons.

"Are You Bisexual?"

But I was so much more than just two.

As I graduated from the blush of pointe shoes to silver stilettos, I bifurcated and proliferated across other dance floors. Skipping chemistry class to visit a stripper called Erica with translucent snake eyes whom I'd pay to wind across my lap as I read her the poems I'd made for her. Spinning at the center of every queer club floor, where the mirror ball morphed the straight lines into liquid. *The winds are blowing every morning / Just to do her hair now / La da dee, La dee da.*

Wherever I turned in the funhouse of flexible selves, Gemini was present on the tip of my tongue, awaiting translation. It began speaking before I could even hold a pen, as my Sesame

Street–inspired fingers slid chunky letter magnets across the side of the fridge. There were no limits to this language, only a movable rainbow of unexpected meet-ups between shapes. After I learned how to take more formal dictation, I'd twirl around the block with my Gemini Sun best friend from across the street, plucking poetics out of the air like soap bubbles and racing back home to transcribe their prismatic shimmers onto Trapper Keeper paper before they popped.

When I let it move through me without forcing it to linger, Gemini multiplied the languages of love. As I grew up, Gemini companions would instantly alight at moments of my meta-morphosis, timed perfectly across each threshold. They'd escort me through loves that lasted for years and in the looks of love that lost their light by dawn. Butterfly love lives. Cat love lives. Swan love lives. When people asked me what I wanted from a relationship, I could only speak in Gemini. There wasn't anything I could possibly want. There were only more and more ways for communion to become me.

After the breakdown, when my body was almost back from near-dust to bone again, a pair of Gemini partners, one Sun and one Moon, were waiting to whisk me the rest of the way. Right on time, in the center of Gemini season, these ushers arrived at an actual staging of *A Midsummer Night's Dream*: the consummate Gemini production of mischief and wings. The matinee turned to midnight and, half-masked, I tumbled in and out of the beds of half the cast. But this wasn't the burn-through-it bacchanal of my Aries stellium or even the bodily bounty of Taurus's please-touch. Instead, it was a breathing through bodies. Alighting, caressing, and leaving changed. *Trip away. Make no stay.*

I sometimes wonder what I can hold on to from these holograms. Where do all the Geminis go? But here they are, once again, speaking from another side. Never the weighted promise of staying from here until the very end, but instead the lifting and leading from here to there and there. *She walked in through the out door, out door*, sings Gemini par excellence Prince.

Now, as my bones start to grow brittle with middle age, they are still bendable, becoming other in their second adolescence. Shape-shifting to pass through another door to a different dance. And with Colorforms that are still filled with more breath, I await Gemini's next invitation to cross the floor.

Beholding Gemini: Catching the Breath

To intercept Gemini's current, you can start by noticing *how things lift and levitate*. Watch a breeze bopping paper bags down the street. Kids being plucked into adult arms, spun, and returned to the ground, changed. The Doppler-effect arrival of the ice-cream truck. A quick kiss on the cheek between some form of friends at an intersection. Gemini energy meets life's multivalence, showing up at street markets, on mixtapes, and atop tapas platters.

Next, let the Gemini current do its work on you:

Consider the in medias res quality of the world as you awaken into its already unfolding tableau. Watch color-changing cars whizzing past the window. Birds flitting from branch to branch, suspended in midair before they're spirited away. Notice the buzz and hum of life caught mid-conversation. Discover how nothing is really all one thing or all the other—follow the second-by-second shape-shifts between the first alarm and the snooze button: your chameleon-like thoughts, particles of dust in the changing light, the cracks in the blinds catching a breath of air.

As you travel to the kitchen, consider the combos in your cabinets that could be double- or triple-dipped. A leftover slice of something drizzled with a sauce packet. A sprinkle of this. A dash of that. A mix-and-mingle inside your mouth. Come alive to the communions you could kick off within you simply by facilitating an elemental exchange between diverse flavors.

Choose clothing that renders you available for life to arrive in many forms. Adjustable straps. A hat or jewel that could shift your whole look in an instant. Stretchy fabrics and sneakers fit for sliding on into the mix, no matter what you meet. When you catch a glimmer of yourself in the mirror, notice what has mood-ringed in your matter at this moment. Do your eyes look more blue than green today? When did that freckle arrive on your face?

Channeling Gemini: Mediuming Your Magic

From Taurus's densely packed earth of plenty, Gemini's air cross-pollinates. The air element is moving around us for the first time. Things blow in, things blow out, and we flow with the breath.

Gemini is **Mutable Air**. Mutable energy morphs and multiplies. It accompanies us as we adapt to changing conditions, reminding us that we are not always fully aware of the effect we have on the world or the effect it has on us. Gemini is our ephemeral escort; it arrives from the wings and walks us down the road a little way.

This is the final sign in the first seasonal trinity of original animation: Aries alives us. Taurus lives us well. And Gemini breathes our life into more forms.

Begin with the double-doored **Gemini glyph**. A portal. A passageway. A meeting point under the mistletoe. Two-ness that connects and communes under an arbor without fully fusing. An appointment to receive the lightest of touches before leaving.

Having glided across this symbol, you can then feel for the presence or absence of **Gemini planets in your birth chart**. Notice both the featheriness where these planets flutter and the weightier places that might be in need of their wings.

From here, fan out into Gemini's facets by exploring its family of associated planets and cards.

Mercury: Your Antenna

Gemini's ruling planet, Mercury, is the conduit that spirits life through us. Governing so much more than just the realm of "communication," this planet speaks to us of all acts of translation: how we pick up, process, and reform what we respire, and change both ourselves and the matter we meet through each exchange.

In Mars, we put out. In Venus, we take up. And in Mercury, we let through. This is the liminal planet that presides over thresholds, crossings, and malleable moments. When we harness its energy, we learn to pay attention to what meets us and to keep whatever it is flexible as it metamorphoses along with us.

Start by asking yourself:

What kind of alchemist am I? How do things come to me—interceptions, inspirations, perceptions? And how do things come through me—when materials, ideas, experiences, and relationships pass through my portal, how do we both change?

Then, you can dive deeper and explore your own Mercury sign. Breathe into the buoyancy of your Mercury sign and its element and inquire:

What would it feel like to translate life through this sign and its element—picking up and sending out messages through its medium?

You can use these conduits for inspiration:

Mercury in Fire (Aries/Leo/Sagittarius) *The Boombox.* Attuning yourself to what's most vibrant and epic in your environment, and using your channel to amplify and cheerlead the matter that moves through you.

Earth (Taurus/Virgo/Capricorn) *The Sieve.* Attuning yourself to what's most beautiful and useful, and using your channel to support and fortify the matter that moves through you.

Air (Gemini/Libra/Aquarius) *The Prism.* Attuning yourself to what's most aspirational and spacious, and using your channel to elevate and circulate the matter that moves through you.

Water (Cancer/Scorpio/Pisces) *The Sponge.* Attuning yourself to what's most empathetic and internal, and using your channel to heal and release the matter that moves through you.

The Magician and the Lovers:
Your Butterfly Effect

These Gemini cards invite us to put ourselves in the line of life and keep the appointments that come calling. In the **Magician**, we attune ourselves for the arrivals: opening our channel to move inspiration and experience through us. And in the **Lovers**, we participate in the exchange: learning to trust that what is meeting us is meant to make some kind of magic with us, for however many moments we both have.

When exploring the Magician, ask yourself:

Where is my attention being drawn? What am I anticipating right now? How can I adopt a posture of openness toward the many forms it may take as it arrives?

How is my creative energy called forth—what does the moment before I make or do something look and feel like? How do I await the arrival of inspiration, and once it's here, how do I harness it?

When exploring the Lovers, ask yourself:

What is meeting me right now, and how am I meeting it? What might this meeting mean, for both me and the other parties?

How can I open up to more mutuality? How can I understand more of the exchange that's present here? How am I being escorted, and what am I escorting?

Divining Gemini: The Art of Becoming

In a world before the arrival of elevated Gemini energy, our firefly attention spans feed on facts without metabolizing their feeling. The ephemeral becomes expendable, and it all seems destined to disappear before we've even considered it. Life's multiplicity of forms trends frivolous and frenetic, and nothing gets the chance to actually take shape.

At one extreme, Gemini energy becomes a distractible dilettante—so eager to stay young and spry in the in-between that any maturation is stunted. And at the other extreme, with a dearth of Gemini, we suffocate—losing all touch with our ability to change into something other or make something else out of what's here.

When wielded consciously, Gemini's greatest gift is **the art of becoming**. We let life through our revolving doors without controlling the final outcomes or fixed forms. And we pay full attention to these passages: befriending what meets us and seeing where it leads us. Experienced in this way, Gemini becomes a balm of buoyancy that frees up our hard notions of "what it is" and "what it means" and lets each meet-and-greet multiply life's possibilities.

A Gemini future asks us to embrace respiration, exchange, and metamorphosis.

Respiration

As experiences arrive, we inhale, let them through us, and exhale. We pay close attention to our portals of perception and explore the balance of what, and how much, we let in; how we process it; and in what forms we put it back out. We understand that all life experiences are interpretive acts, and we examine our critical role in shaping the matter that moves through our conduits into something else that some other entity will breathe in. We celebrate levity and circulation, and divest from the notion that the only things that have value are those with solidity and clear definition. We keep life permeable by breathing either/ors into three-or-mores.

Exchange

We embrace the rainbow of relationships in its greatest range. No matter the declared commitments or defined containers, we celebrate all encounters as inherently ephemeral and no more or less meaningful for their relative durations. We welcome more visitors to pass through our doors, and we consciously put ourselves in the line of more forms of life by challenging our beliefs about the people, places, and ideas that are, or are not, "for" us. We are open to the possibility that there is always reciprocity in a relationship, no matter the roles assigned or even the relative power apportioned. We acknowledge that we can never really know who we are meant to be for another being, or who they're meant to be for us. And we allow for as many meanings to be made out of each encounter as possible.

Metamorphosis

We let the liminal live. We mark and honor the in-between and the not-yet-formed, and we actively inhabit the spaces between here and there, this and that. We accompany one another across thresholds. And we allow whoever and whatever is before us to change before our very eyes, without forcing them into a form that upholds our expectations or even serves our needs. We let each other change names, places, identifications, presentations, roles, and agreements. And we let ourselves be changed by, through, and with others' changes. We no longer have to hold life to a static standard, or declare what something is or is not, in order to value it as fully real and absolutely worthy of love.

Sheltering + Returning

From the belly of the basement, my Moon-in-Cancer mother's calls came seeping through the vents. *Elizabeth? Elizabeth? Are you still there?*

Cordoned off in my bedroom as a child, crafting choreography for the fiery life that would one day free me from the ivy that crept through the screen, I was determined to remain beyond her reach. I'd resist my response to her calls for as long as I could. My safety lay in the separateness of self. The refusal to answer to the way she said my name.

But for her, the safest self was spongy. Speaking through the cracks in the floorboards, her heart haunted our house with its humidity, corroding the lock off my bedroom door in the name of her love. There was no place she couldn't pour. Even the wallpaper sweated her scent of waterlogged lilies like the amniotic inside of an oyster.

She'd been born to two Cancer Suns. Mom Mom "Missy" and Pop Pop "TJ" were centrifugal forces at high tide holding highball glasses. Legends in a small town, they'd become homing devices in a family-built model of Pop Pop's ancestral Irish village on an American street behind a 7–11. Each abode on "Nenagh Drive" held a relation in its locket: brothers, sisters, fathers, mothers, and cousins all archipelago'ed like a string of pearls. With Missy and TJ's back-to-back birthdays leading up to the Fourth of July, we grandkids would compete to claim the coveted role of blender master for another endless summer of cracked-egg whiskey sours.

Each Cancer season, the in-ground pool party behind the house, with its flat rubber sharks and succubus of a deep-end drain, would try to claim a life. Little kids from the neighborhood with deflating water wings, bobbing in and out of the blue as the grownups poured another and another and another, oblivious. And Miss Missy herself, who'd never been taught to swim, weaving along the cement edge and then backwards into the chlorine. We speared her back to dry land with the metal net we'd use to skim the bottle-green flies that could have killed her just as easily.

Years later, Missy would die in the center of Cancer season while I kept the floodlight on in the deep end of the pool past midnight. And in a Cancer season years after she'd shed her shell, I'd answer another call from home. From a pay phone on a labyrinthine street in Barcelona, my mother's voice came through the line once again, telling the story of a saltwater sadness that would have no end. Her baby brother—the one who was so much younger than she that he could have come from her body—had soaked his bloodstream in booze, fled her double-wide beach trailer at sunset, and jumped the median on a coastal highway. Head-on with a cop car, he'd killed them both. The last song he'd penned, called "Pour It On," soundtracked his wake.

Half a world away from home, there was nowhere for me to go but down to the water's edge. Accompanied by my slippery Venus-in-Cancer lover, who'd been raised in a South Bronx highrise and couldn't swim, I dove in. I was pulled straight under after just a few strokes, caught in a riptide. Tiny pebbles filled my mouth and nose. Each time I broke the surface, I was no longer fit to breathe. Over and over again, as my sea-leg-less lover receded along the distant sand, I choked and sputtered on the story of salt. This was it. My flame was going to be put out. But at the final moment, somehow, I remembered how to swim parallel to the shore.

Twenty years later, yet another Cancer season called me back. My now-septuagenarian mother's basement flooded, sending me sloshing home to help her dry all the dampness out of its bones. I found the room where our family memories were stored inundated with a drenched history that dripped from the pages down toward the storm drain. Cardboard chests of love letters soaked through to see through. Photo negatives melting into sorbet swirl as my rubber-gloved hands tried to hold them. Tiny childhood toys surfing the break, riding the waves astride the beetled backs of giant water bugs.

Up in bed past midnight, my mother's floating fantasy land came alive. She dreamed magically real trips back to her source and story-told them to me in the morning. The thinnest layers of sashimi secreted within the frame of one of my father's

Amish paintings. A cousin laid out in a coffin styled after her zucchini-shaped ceramic butter dish. Fat frogs falling from the ceiling that her father tried to capture. During the daylight, with hooded eyes half open, she'd read death dates and birth dates from her this-day-in-our-history spiral-bound notebook and disappear into the cinematic cocoon of others' lives on the television screen.

What could I know of her waterlogged worlds within? In my own birth chart, I don't have a drop to drink. Cancer appears as an *interception*: a swallowed space with no door in, no door out, and no planet to keep it company inside. My whole life, I'd held out against this sign's sea of love. Tried to hold fast to my scrap of dry land.

I'd been determined to come from nothing. To big-bang my own birth, Aries style. But in the flooded basement, I found that I came from nothing but Cancer. My body, and the bodies of my mother and her mother, Cancer Moon and Cancer Sun, became wet nesting dolls bobbing along the surface of our family swimming pool. Half-floating, half-sinking, like suspended Fabergé eggs.

How could I think that I could ever fight their tide when I'd been conceived by it this whole time?

Beholding Cancer: Bringing It In

To crest Cancer's current, start by noticing *how things find their way inside*. Explore the homing devices that return each being to the fold of its feelings. The washing out and return of shell shapes at the water's edge. Apartment lights flickering to life at dusk as dwellers roll back toward their own deep. Kids reeling from street to front door, timed to invisible dinner bells. Dumplings gathering and pleating their goods within.

Next, let the Cancer current do its work on you:

Begin your day by exploring the parcel from which you emerge. Maybe the blankets were flung to the floor overnight and now you're stripped clean. Or maybe you're thoroughly bundled and cushioned. Curl deeper in before you climb out, padding yourself in comforters and possibly even rolling from bed to floor like a sleeping samosa.

Notice the wrappings that surround you. Plexiglas protecting picture-framed memories. Crown molding and book covers. Everything is a tender present, sanctified with ceremonious enveloping. Become aware of the boomerang that brings life home before heading out again. Idling engines warming up in the driveway. Taking a shower back to the source of life before you descend the staircase.

Select snacks that will take in, surround, and protect themselves and your body. Pour contents into and out of deep cereal bowls, mugs, ladles, and jugs. Nestle your fork in French toast crannies that provide hotel-like harbors for thick, liquid syrup.

Consider the conceal and reveal of your clothing. Maybe you're ready to come out uncovered, in a crop top. Or maybe you're craving the cover-up of a hoodie. As you catch a glimpse of your eyes in the mirror, notice what looks back with familiar feeling. The lines your face has settled into before and has found once again. And the lines that are part of your familial line.

Channeling Cancer: Protecting Your Realm

Moving from Gemini's in-out breath, Cancer inhales us down into the bowl of our being. The water element is welcoming us for the first time, surrounding and inundating us with its slipperiness and its salt. The current calls, and we come inside.

Cancer is **Cardinal Water**. All cardinal energy champions its element, and here in water, Cancer guards the mouth of the cove—the sanctified spaces within us that need covering. Cancer's water conceives us and returns us. We are born from it, and we come back to it.

This is the first sign in the second seasonal trinity of Cancer-Leo-Virgo. After the sheer aliveness of our first season's trio, this is the keepsake trinity: as we travel through its signs, we clasp life close to our chest and find our special place within it.

Begin with the jelly bracelet of **Cancer's glyph**. An inherited heirloom slipped onto a wrist. A beaded clutch made of caviar carried into the night. The curled-up origins of life as they incubate in the inchoate.

Sheltered by this symbol, you can then feel for the presence or absence of **Cancer planets in your birth chart**. Notice both the shaded spaces that hold these planets and the more exposed places that live without their shell.

From here, fan out into Cancer's facets by exploring its family of associated planets and cards.

The Moon: Your Source

Cancer's ruling celestial body, the Moon, is our hideaway and home turf. An instinctual pull into our interior, it is the lagoon from which we emerge and the shell-shaped purse that cushions our softest parts. Everywhere we go, we bring its emotional weather with us. And everywhere we go, we must find ways to feed it well, so that we always have a home away from home.

Start by asking yourself:

Where do I come from? What do I belong to? What are my core needs for survival? What protects me? What do I reveal? And what do I hide?

Then, you can dive deeper and explore your own Moon sign. Welcome yourself into the enclosure of this sign and its element, inquiring:

What are my earliest memories of this sign and element — maybe even from existences before this one? How does it feel to emerge out of its atmosphere? How can I trust that it's always safe inside me?

You can use these habitats for inspiration:

- **Moon in Fire (Aries/Leo/Sagittarius)** *The Hearth*. Returning to the source of life's brazen heart, and supporting yourself through earnest emotional sharing and passionate pledges.
- **Earth (Taurus/Virgo/Capricorn)** *The Foundation*. Returning to the source of life's solid bones, and supporting yourself by giving finite form to feelings and staying with them through time.
- **Air (Gemini/Libra/Aquarius)** *The Foyer*. Returning to the source of life's capacious lungs, and supporting yourself by breathing through emotions and letting them locomote.
- **Water (Cancer/Scorpio/Pisces)** *The Bathtub*. Returning to the source of life's shared liquid, and supporting your-

self by feeding your fantasies and plunging into personal sensations before you express them to others.

The High Priestess and the Chariot: Your Home and Away

These Cancer cards invite us into the sanctuaries that shelter us. In the **High Priestess**, we travel into our interior, heading from the outside in as we follow our deepest conch-shell callings. And in the **Chariot**, we learn to come out from the inside, shedding the shell of defenses that keep us cloistered from life and heeding calls to come of age.

When exploring the High Priestess, ask yourself:

How do I go inside of myself? What calls me back to myself? What are my natural rhythms? What does silence sound like to me, and how does this silence speak?

How do I listen to myself? How does intuitive knowing come to me—through images, sounds, tastes, smells, feelings . . . ? When have I followed this knowing? Why, and where has it led? When have I deviated from it? Why, and where has this led?

When exploring the Chariot, ask yourself:

How do I cover myself? What pads me from the roughness of living? What are my defense mechanisms and comfort zones, and what do they serve to protect? Which of these defenses support my life? And which of them are good and done?

What era of my life am I in right now? Where am I being asked to grow up and move on? How can I caretake myself through my own coming of age?

Divining Cancer: The Art of Incubating

In a world before the arrival of elevated Cancer energy, we give birth to half-baked creations and immediately force everything into the harsh light of day. We push projects, share statuses, and coerce conversations before they're seaworthy, and we preserve nothing for the safe harbor of our hearts.

At one extreme, Cancer energy refuses to relinquish its baby blankets and grow its own backbone, as it stews in preserved hurts and hopes without ever leaving home. And at the other extreme, with a dearth of Cancer, we turn our home-sweet-homes inside out, forgoing any caretaking of our interior and cutting the phone line to our inner knowing in the process.

When wielded consciously, Cancer's greatest gift is **the art of incubating**. This is the shaded space where things are allowed to exist and grow inside the shell that best sanctifies their soft shape: gaining strength from an inner source, taking good care of their deepest selves, and getting a feel for their own feelings before they're fed to the world. Here, Cancer becomes a balm of eternal return, where we can protect the inchoate, honor our sources, and come back home whenever we need a safe place to land.

A Cancer future asks us to embrace protection, remembrance, and belonging.

Protection

We commit to creating sanctuaries where diverse forms of life can grow at their own rates and according to their own needs. We honor a range of gestation periods for ideas, emotions, projects, and partnerships. And we sensitize ourselves to differing rhythms of concealing and revealing. This means

inquiring into both the defenses that guard life and the impe-
tuses behind acts of exposure. We explore our own comfort
zones and growing edges, then how ours intersect with those
of others. We recognize that sometimes we'll need to move out
of our comfort zone to shelter others. And at other times, we'll
need to advocate for our own emotional protection, even if it
challenges another's comfort.

Remembrance

Without fetishizing families of origin or bloodlines, we seek
to understand the sources of our life: the emotional contexts
and climates through which we are created and of which we are
forever a part. We excavate both visible and invisible histories:
how we are shaped both by what we've seen and who we've met,
and by what we've never seen and who we've never met. We
also honor the autonomy of memory: Shared experiences do
not create the same souvenirs, and we are the ultimate keepers
of what holds meaning in our personal history.

Belonging

We commit to creating and sustaining communities of care that
accept and accommodate a multitude of life-forms and help
them find a home here on earth. This means giving both our
hard-to-love parts and our easy-to-love parts a place to land.
We envision caregiving as a shifting symbiosis of interdepen-
dence rather than an imbalanced codependency. We hold the
balance between belonging to ourselves and sharing this self
with others. And we ensure that someone is "home" inside of
our self to hold us safe before we outsource our desire for connection and attachment to any other.

Baring + Romancing

My Leo Moon shone all the way from my head through my toes as I beheld my very own feet in their brand-new pair of jellies. These were the kitten-heeled kind that turned kids' tea parties into make-believe cocktail hours. The kind I'd been coveting since I'd first seen Effie Pappas pull her plasticky pair of salmon pink ones out of her cubbyhole and turn herself into a pint-sized star with a click of her heels.

I had held their latticed image close to my chest like a lacey Valentine for so long. And now they were mine at last! Inside the brown box on the discounted back racks at Value City, they'd only had the white ones left. The color of a chalky Lik-M-Aid stick after it had been licked. But by god, were they glorious.

Alone in the backyard, I stretched one leg long, then the other, like a slow-motion Rockette swimming through the high summer heat. And as I turned and turned to catch the orange-blossom light, my Cinderella slippers became so much more than a put-on costume piece. In beholding my being beholding them right back, their beauty became me. Fantasy made flesh.

With my jellies fused to my feet, my Leo Moon's love story lived larger than life. I found it in the fat romance paperbacks plucked from the creaky dust of the rotating rack. In the furry stickers pressed onto my Trapper Keeper, never to be traded. When tasked with the oppressive gray matter of everything from math drills to making the bed (hospital corners!), I was reborn as an actress named Lilac Moore starring as Bess Matassa in the soap operatic glory of a show called *Life*. Complete with a theme song that played on loop in my head, I'd leave an autograph of hot pink puffy paint on whatever less-than-royal life to-do I had to wrangle.

Everywhere I turned, life could be made into more of itself simply by looking at it through the eyes of adoration. Wherever I roamed and whatever I romanced, my Leo Moon never left me. Even before I'd become flesh and blood, this Moon had conceived of me in full color. It had warmed up the hot plate for me to take my place at its center. And its heart would go on long after my body had grown cold.

It was with me as I bedazzled jean jackets and flashed jazz hands to Paula Abdul's "Forever Your Girl." It was with me as I planned fantasy weddings in Vegas and honeymoons in Maui with my latest lover. It was roller-skating to my forty-eight-hour-long "Weddings & Funerals" playlist (which was fit for exalting the epicness of my life in the event either of a union or of my demise). My bigness would keep the beat whether or not I'd be here in body (but surely I would, because somehow, the specialness of my sparkle would render me the first person never ever to die).

And long after I outgrew my Lik-M-Aid slipperettes, it was with me as I slid my feet into a pair of now adult-sized jellies. They were a shade of lilac befitting Ms. Moore of *Life* fame. In them, I now stood beside the smallest grave I'd ever seen.

It was last rites for a meant-to-be Leo Sun baby who hadn't even taken a breath, born still through the voluptuous body of a beloved Taurus friend. This Taurus and I had been twinned through the life-death dance. My Sicilian father's death date was her birthday. And her Neapolitan dad's death had happened on mine. Together, we went after the sweet cream center of our still-hereness like it was a silver platter of sfogliatelle served after a South Brooklyn funeral supper.

She'd been by my side as I'd been whisked out of the shadow of my own death in these adult-sized lilac mini-heels. And now I stood by hers, in the same slippers, facing a coffin not much bigger than a Polly Pocket compact. On that day, the dirt in the hole was denser and darker than all the matter I'd tried to make more-than with my Leo Moon. Thick, dry chocolate clumps that could catch in your throat and bring you all the way down.

How could we possibly fill it? How could we not lose heart?

Yet all the way down in the center of that impenetrable earth, riding astride the casket like a cake topper, we'd placed a tiny stuffed lion. Upright and exultant from mane to tail. And as the priest summoned us to start our scatter, we grabbed fistfuls of that thickness and I felt its humus heartbeat inside my own clenched hand.

Our fistfuls rained down on that little lion's plush body, burying it alive, bit by bit. And then, somehow, at the last second, it started to turn softer. The fistfuls of dirt catching its fur like sun freckles, bejeweling the body of its being. Glowing in the face of the coldest blood, its tawny gold was still warm, warmer, warmest.

And so were we.

Yes, it would all end. But Leo was still a love story, all the way to the end.

Beholding Leo: Taking Heart

To clutch Leo's current closer, you can start by noticing *how things become beloved*: magnified into more of themselves through moments of adoration. Stacks of juicy fruit in the supermarket, ripening up for the pleasure of your pluck. A compliment given freely to a stranger that disarms in an instant. A confident claim to a color that brings your skin tone into relaxed resplendence. In the Leo lifeworld, each being is a protagonist in a grand romance that can turn even the tiniest flower faces toward the warmth of their willingness to come forward.

Next, let the Leo current do its work on you:

Begin your day by regarding your remarkable form. Notice the natural flair that distinguishes you from any other mere slogger getting up for another day on earth. A cherished memory of a dream only you could have dreamed. The bespokeness of your bedroom style. As you bring your body alive, gaze upon each part and watch how it responds to your attention. The dignity of a foot stepping out. The flutter of lashes lifting. Unclench your chest as you uncurl from the sheets, and broaden and emblazon the space across your heart.

Notice how everything in the room awaits you. A parched plant turning toward you for a drink. A beloved pet at the foot of the bed expecting morning bites fed from your palm. Even an unsent email poised to love-letter its way toward a ready recipient. Imagine how, rather than a to-do list of duties, the day's agenda can feel like invitations for a playdate sent out to willing parties.

Let your breakfast snacks come forward and show themselves. The pop of a box lid that sends cereal celebrating its own sprinkle into the bowl. A whistling tea kettle making its warm readiness well known. Give your food your regard and bear witness to its presentation just before you take a bite.

Amplify an aspect of your being that you find beautiful by playing up this part of you, even if the act is as miniscule as gifting your pinky finger a nail decal. Add elements that feel "extra" and let them nestle into the naturalness of you: blot lipstick until it settles deeper onto your mouth, braid a clip-in hairpiece into the fold of your existing mane, or let a tie or jewelry piece settle into the contours of your skin. Come toward your face in the mirror, closer and closer, until the surrounding scene falls away.

Channeling Leo: Gifting Your Glow

Out of Cancer's shaded cove, we emerge into the generous gleam of Leo's high noon. The fire element is welcoming us for the second time. In Aries' fire, we essentialized our existence and left a dent. Now, we exalt in the larger-than-life and bedazzle our dent into a pawprint.

Leo is **Fixed Fire**. Fixed energy remains constant through cycles of having and losing. In Leo, we learn to sunbathe, bringing our presence forward earnestly and candidly, without fearing that the stuff we're made of will ever run out.

This is the second sign in the second seasonal trinity of Cancer-Leo-Virgo, where we make a home inside our own hearts. We encircle what we love in Cancer. And we love it louder in Leo. The road ahead through the second half of the zodiac—from Libra all the way to Pisces—will be long and weathered, and it will challenge our love of life. Here in Leo, we must stay courageously warm, so that we're ready for the seasons when life grows colder.

Begin with the glamorama of **Leo's glyph.** Part playground equipment, part hairdo. A ringlet on holiday. A cherry-on-top sundae with a high ponytail. An invitation to monogram your majesty.

Bejeweled by this symbol, you can then feel for the presence or absence of **Leo planets in your birth chart.** Notice both the places where these planets shine and the spots their sun doesn't yet reach.

From here, fan out into Leo's facets by exploring its family of associated planets and cards.

The Sun: Your Presence Is Requested

Leo's ruling celestial body, the Sun, is our essence made conscious: we are both born as already-realized perfections of our Sun sign's fundamental qualities and on a mission to recover the center of this sign's heart.

While the Moon's powerful pull cannot be repressed, the Sun's clarion call cannot be ignored. When we deny our Sun, we deny our self, and our life loses its light and meaning. And when we answer the Sun's call, it is our most courageous act of individuation. We stand up, stand out, and stand alone, risking separateness by becoming more of what we already are.

Start by asking yourself:

Who is the me who's been here through it all, all along? What are the qualities that I cannot deny, no matter what it costs to show them? What brings me into presence? If I could use just one word to describe my essence, what would it be?

Then, you can dive deeper and explore your own Sun sign.

While there are millions of beings born under each of the twelve signs, each of us has incarnated to leave our distinctive mark on our Sun sign's turf—forever changing some aspect of this archetype simply by living in its light. No one can do our Sun quite like we can. And our life's work is to divine the one tiny tweak or grand flourish that will unequivocally evidence that we were indeed "here" to inhabit our sign.

Probe this personalization process:

How can I harness the energy of my Sun sign, and its element, in order to become more of myself? And how can I make this sign more mine? What never-before-seen aspects of it can only I bring forward?

You can use these glows for inspiration:

- **Sun in Fire (Aries/Leo/Sagittarius)** *Incandescence*. Becoming more present with your warmth, passion, bravery, and innocence.
- **Earth Signs (Taurus/Virgo/Capricorn)** *Florescence*. Becoming more present with your commitment, timelessness, worth, and resourcefulness.

Air Signs (Gemini/Libra/Aquarius) *Effervescence*. Becoming more present with your perspective, vision, insight, and inventiveness.

Water Signs (Cancer/Scorpio/Pisces) *Iridescence*. Becoming more present with your imagination, perceptiveness, magnetism, and responsiveness.

Strength and the Sun: Your See-and-Be-Seen

These Leo cards are show-it-to-grow-it: here to bring us closer to life's heartbeat without barriers and to help us revel in skin-to-skin contact with this sensational world. In the **Strength** card, we show ourselves to life—coming forward in warmth, without defense or pretense. And in the **Sun**, we let life show itself to us—allowing the power of solar presence to reveal things exactly as they are, without equivocation or complication.

When exploring Strength, ask yourself:

How could I become barer? What does vulnerability look like for me?

What are my fears around coming forward and showing my cards? What one act of going first might help soften a situation?

When exploring the Sun, ask yourself:

What is showing itself to me, and how am I showing up for it? How could letting something be just as it is help me, and it, to become more of ourselves?

If I could reduce this life moment to just a few words or feelings, what would they be? What is the simplest solution or most uncomplicated approach?

Divining Leo: The Art of Dignifying

In a world before the arrival of elevated Leo energy, we struggle with proportion. At one extreme, Leo energy blimps into me-first megalomania, so caught up in the personal that its self-absorbed sparkle eclipses everything that surrounds it. And at the other extreme, with a dearth of Leo, we become charisma-less smudges who blindly adhere to the cult of self-lessness, so frightened of our own magnificence that our life becomes DOA.

When wielded consciously, Leo's greatest gift is **the art of dignifying**. As we pour the largesse of our love out from the center of a stable self, both we and the objects of our adoration naturally plump up. We are proud to hold them, they are proud to be held, and we are both ready to reveal more of our realness through a generous see-and-be-seen. Experienced in this way, Leo becomes a colorful balm against cynicism that makes all the gray matter worth living, and a call for every creature to come forward without guile and share more of its specialness.

A Leo future asks us to embrace courage, magnanimity, and splendor.

Courage

We commit to showing more of our true selves to life and, in turn, to letting life show more of itself to us. This means risking the exposure of our tenderness and staying open and available to let experiences and people in, even in the face of apathy and past hurt. This exposure is born not from a blind naivete or a self-punitive wish to retraumatize, but from the knowledge that even if we hold back, our hearts can break just the same. When we commit to coming forward in the face of whatever faces us, we have only more of our own hearts to gain.

Magnanimity

We honor the infinity loop of generosity, where beaming out more of our brightness into the world and onto others gives both of us a glow. We each have the power to become the Sun for something or someone. This means pouring forth into our projects, passions, and partnerships not from expectation, obligation, or responsibility, but first and foremost from the enjoyment of our own essence. This is the power of our presence: By our simply showing up and staying warm, life grows under our gaze.

Splendor

We exalt the epicness of this life and embrace its inherent dramatics. We expand our definition of romance to include the infusion of the glamorous, magical, and megawatt into the mundane. We emphasize and enhance the singularity and vividness of our experiences, and celebrate each other's personal successes, passions, hopes, and heartfelt dreams, however small or gargantuan. We go big and over-the-top together and rejoice in giving each other more of our god-given glory.

Virgo

Supplicating + Devoting

I traced Virgo to my father's studio and found its door sealed shut. I could sense the presence of the process behind it. Soft lead tips shading. Metallic rulers finding their level. The subtlest swishes across canvas. The sounds I knew must have sprung from the tiny brushes whose ghostly swirls I'd see in the bathroom sink we shared. A mandala whose meaning I tried to discern before it melted down the drain.

I'd pad softly to that closed door, hover my ear just outside, and hold my breath. If I stayed still enough, I could hear those brushes breathing the world into being. Left to their own devices, the creations revealed themselves through a crack. Intricately crafted universes on their own terms and timelines, these works were wed to the weather of someone else's withinness that I could witness but never possess.

My Virgo Sun father had always told me that if things went south, he'd choose his own way to die. And he did. Faced with a wall of accusations that would likely land him behind bars, he was discovered near the river by a stranger out walking their dog at dawn. The rifle had removed his head, so we identified him by the hands that had held his instruments. His letter revealed that by the time of its reading, he would already have become a bird. *Just look up, wait, and watch the sky.*

I scattered his cremains all the way from wintertime on Coney Island, when the kiddie rides cuddled under tarps, to the springtime of volcanic soil in Sicily, where the shutters were secrets that spoke my family name. I even swallowed some of them: determined somehow to make him more mine by taking his body into my bones. But he remained inscrutable and apart past his end: I unconsciously knocked his final urn of ashes off my nightstand and into the bin. The next morning, it was taken out with the trash.

After the basement flooded, his paintings finally gave in and gave themselves over, edged in a fine fur of black mold. I carefully pried the papers apart and found an entire family of roaches sleeping between the sheets. Inside one portfolio, a mother bug gave birth straight onto the canvas, dedicating his labor to the world through hers. He was a precious part of every piece, at last.

Years later, I met my own Virgo, and it brought me to my knees.

It started with the subtlest of signs: a glossy bump on my scalp the size of a popcorn kernel, nestled like a gold nugget within the forest of wavy dark locks that were my crowning glory. Self-viewing was impossible, so friends scrutinized it from above. They were convinced it was nothing more than a stubborn pimple.

But this pore soon proved to be the portal into a sci-fi spectacular, and within a month my entire head was covered in massive waxy growths, some as big as my palm. The skin doctors had never seen the likes of them before, but they were determined to treat them like any other interloper: injecting each monstrous mountain with steroids until it ripped halfway off my head like a dinosaur spike.

The more furiously I focused on tearing my scalp bare so that I could get over whatever this was and get on with my planned head tattoo of a tiger, the more my body whispered: *I am not a battlefield but a thing of strange beauty*. What if there was no problem? No aberration of "wellness" or illness in need of interception? And maybe even no reason why? What if there was only the reality of being in a body, in time, and letting it talk?

I abandoned the steroids, scrubs, and search for answers, and bowed my head each night instead—sliding layers of skin away from the surface only as they were ready to slip. The removal of each sci-fi sheet took a chest-length section of my locks with it, from root to tip. As I flushed these primordial-looking dolls down the drain, I'd say out loud to each: *Thank you for your service. We're clearing the way.*

Stripped of the Leo Moon lion's mane that I believed was my only real marker of physical beauty, my face changed. My eyes became wider, my shoulders more supple. I could see all of my skin.

Instead of wild animal head tats, I donned head wraps. On the train, strangers stole glances with heavy, sad eyes, assuming my terminal fate. In my neighborhood, I blended seamlessly into the crowds of Muslim women at the market. And as I wandered the Met's sarcophagi on Friday nights, the trace of my father's Egyptian ancestry animated something ancient in me, summoning a call-and-response from each amulet: *What is eternal? It isn't hair.*

In my birth chart, all my Aries planets are packed into the Virgo-ruled sixth house. They are learning to follow the Virgoan ways. As each sheet of skin slid off, I slid to my knees and submitted, contemporaneously partnered in a BDSM relationship that charted the course of my curvature precisely. Folding into my present form instead of fighting against it, I saw the future and intuited that the final mass would be peeled by Aries season.

Right on time, just before the start of the astrological new year in March 2020, I was finally bare enough to be shaved into a bald baby chick. My unwrapped skull soaked up all the early spring sunlight it could. One week later, we were quarantined. With my studio apartment as my new wrap, I bowed back in and under, knowing that this too would be just another season.

By the time we were released back into the world, a coat of fine fur covered my head. Much softer than before. And even darker. It was the color of my father's hair.

Beholding Virgo: Taking the Shape

To bring Virgo's current into relief, you can start by noticing *how things dedicate themselves*, pledging the particularity of their nature to nature itself. The wild order of the woods with its sacred geometry. An intricate piece of lace. A pasta sieve separating the fusilli. The terroir and viticulture of a grapevine. The processes that unfold inside your body, within an insect colony, and in the vespertine light of dusk.

Next, let the Virgo current do its work on you:

Start by following the morphology of your form as you wake. See how you can both honor the intactness of this original form and also work within it. Bend into a bit of your body that's already curved or inclined in a certain way and take even more of your organic shape.

As you look around you, notice how everything in the room attends its purpose. A lamp that's been off overnight, knowing its time to turn on will come. A pen poised atop a journal, ready to write without rushing. The lamp's non-pen-ness. The pen's non-lamp-ness. Each object summoned to serve by standing alone.

Become reverential in your morning rituals. Notice the internal alchemy of your breakfast, where each chosen bite sends vitamins through your system, depositing its magic and changing you both in the process. Coffee brewed both *by* you and *for* you and also entirely for itself: the beans becoming what they were born to be by grace of your allowing them to fulfill their fruit.

Observe the sartorial order of your room. Maybe each piece of clothing is hung on its own hanger. Or maybe they're tossed into emergent patterns on the back of the chair. Take time to select pieces that will best serve your shape in this moment. Then, see what it might feel like to let them wear you. Respond to their texture and weight. Take on the veil of their color.

Channeling Virgo: Marrying Your Matter

Occupying spot six in our journey of twelve signs, Virgo marks a critical turning point in the soul's development. After reaching the pinnacle of personal power in Leo, when we enter Virgo's temple, we submit to existing at the intersection of our terms and life's terms.

We are welcoming earth for the second time. In Taurus, we learn to be in a body and absorb matter into it. In Virgo, we bow to this body and discern its constituent parts. Virgo is **Mutable Earth**. Mutable energy remains responsive. Virgo is our attendant: awaiting the right moment, yielding to the conditions, and bending without breaking as it becomes wet clay for the world to work.

This is our final sign in the second seasonal trinity of keepsakes, composed of Cancer, Leo, and Virgo. By now, we know the heart of our matter and can give ourselves over to it in the name of our love.

Begin with the intricate integrity of **Virgo's glyph**. Its hills morphing with the weather into a rise and fall without having to flex their will. The coiled-unto-the-self final tuck. A customized lace garter that's neither indiscriminately open nor hermetically sealed shut.

Having sieved this symbol, you can then feel for the presence or absence of **Virgo planets in your birth chart**. Notice the places where these planets curve to the conditions and keep their own counsel and the spaces that could benefit from a bended knee.

From here, fan out into Virgo's facets by exploring its family of associated planets and cards.

Mercury: Your Weathervane

The planet Mercury rules both Gemini and Virgo. Through Virgo's earthiness, we meet Mercury's more metabolic function. Here, we use the planet to digest our experiences, send their nutrition where it serves best, and become well-honed weathervanes who divine when our time is exactly right.

To experience this expression of Mercury, you can start by asking yourself:

How am I processing what's happening? Am I burning through the calories of circumstances like an athlete? Am I slowly taking life's happenings into my bones like a hibernating animal?

Then, you can return to your own Mercury sign and its element and inquire:

How can I use this sign and its element to divine when the time is exactly right? How can I read the seasons of my life through its lens, and respond accordingly?

You can use these seasons for inspiration:

Mercury in Fire (Aries/Leo/Sagittarius) *Spring*. Noticing how the right moment arises through an inevitable burst and push forth that feels innocently lean and green.

Earth (Taurus/Virgo/Capricorn) *Winter*. Noticing how the right moment arises when things begin to land, gaining stronger significance and blanketed weight.

Air (Gemini/Libra/Aquarius) *Autumn*. Noticing how the right moment arises when the light starts to slant toward aspiration, revealing sharper sight lines and clarified contours.

Water (Cancer/Scorpio/Pisces) *Summer*. Noticing how the right moment arises through an allowing and an unwinding of resistance, as release gives rise to response.

Vesta: Your Altar

In addition to this metabolic expression of Mercury, Virgo's honorary asteroid, Vesta, shapes this sign into a vessel. Working with this asteroid helps us to identify the altars that merit our devotion and to remain intact as we offer ourselves up.

To come alive to Vesta's properties, you can start by asking yourself:

What makes me feel whole unto myself? What is my inner code, and how do I pay allegiance to it? What am I wed to? What merits my matter? How and to what do I give myself over?

You can then start to filter these questions through your own Vesta sign's element. (It doesn't appear on most basic astrology charts, so you can search online for "what's my Vesta sign?") Ask yourself:

How can I commit to containing this sign and its element within me, and pouring forth from it on my own terms?

Placed in fire signs, explore how you can give over your life force on your own terms; in earth, your resources; in air, your vision; and in water, your feeling.

The Hermit: Your Table-for-One

Bolstered by its companion card, the Mercury-infused **Magician** —which enlivens our ability to pay close attention—the Virgo-infused **Hermit** card asks us to attend to ourselves and our lives through changing conditions. The Hermit acknowledges the solitude in Virgo's makeup: the specificity of self that is ultimately unrepresentable and untranslatable to others. When we work with this card, we are asked to stay by and on our own side. Through it, we learn to meet our specific self at any given time and to honor our changing role within our own life.

When exploring the Hermit, ask yourself:

Who am I when I am wholly alone? How does this person diverge from the version of me who shows up in company?

Who am I being asked to be "for myself" right now: a fierce advocate, a tender lover, a cool-headed teacher? How can I meet myself where I am and serve my specificity?

Divining Virgo: The Art of Apprenticing

In a world before the arrival of elevated Virgo energy, we either bend the weather to our will or are broken by it. At one extreme, we try to beat the seasons into submission by fixing each bit of minutiae, forgetting the already-finery of each grain of sand. And at the other extreme, we become long-suffering submissives who perform the dirty work without taking any pleasure in dedicating our devotion.

When wielded consciously, Virgo's greatest gift is **the art of apprenticing.** Instead of having to be and do and have it all, we show up willing to learn from life's processes and discover our highly specific form and function. When we stop trying to multi-hyphenate, we become precious parts of an ecosystem where we actually have a place. We're irreplaceable and invaluable treasures both *for* the world and *for* ourselves. Experienced in this way, Virgo becomes a supple balm in a world of nonconsensual power dynamics, where we can give of our gifts because we have the whole of ourselves to give.

A Virgo future asks us to embrace seasonality, discernment, and veneration.

Seasonality

We allow ourselves to be in process, and we give ourselves time and space to digest, assimilate, and integrate experiences. We pay attention and attend to the shifting shapes of ourselves, each other, and current conditions. And we let this attention give rise to the right timing. If we're down, it's time to get down. If we're up, it's time to get on up. Becoming one with the weather of the world, we learn to respond instead of react.

Discernment

We cultivate consciousness around what we consume and take on—not out of a parched asceticism but out of a deep reverence for what our bodies, minds, and hearts can best handle and hold. We understand that we are not meant to have, do, and be it all. We acknowledge the need to support our potential and grant increased access to aspirations for every one of us. And we also learn to identify our capacities and accept our limits. We honor craft and expertise, and we hone the specificity of our purpose here on earth.

Veneration

We enliven our awe for the particular and ritualize the exquisiteness of the everyday. We elevate the unsung efforts that animate the world's woodwork and unfold behind the scenes. While confronting and seeking to dismantle the very real power imbalances that exist in the world, we simultaneously awaken opportunities for consensual supplication and submission. This means identifying the partnerships, projects, passions, and places that are worthy of our prayer: where we experience strong mutual respect and admiration, and where we can then give ourselves over willingly, in sweet devotion.

Libra

Clarifying + Elevating

Libra and I caught each other's eye from across the room.

It all started with elementary school hand-holding with a Libra Sun. An unspoken affinity coupled us beside each other on the bench like perfectly paired lunch meats. Fingers tightly clasped, we dueted during every field trip, and my Aries-ness came into relief against his Libran light. I was scrunchy waves to his slick side part. Candid home videos at my backyard birthday party reeling before his calm, collected gaze.

From this little luminary forward, the Libras lined up to launch me all the way across the zodiac to their other side. Libra was a hoop to jump through. An Aries dare, elevated.

I orchestrated elaborate love triangles for my Libras, designed to provoke them into fighting for my Aries end of the polarity. And they did just the same—counterbalancing my instigations with a cool remove that left me swinging at air.

The Libra stellium affair that dominated my early twenties created a chemical reaction that almost killed us. He launched a potted plant from a fourth-story window in a vain attempt to flatten my force. I drove my station wagon straight into his bedroom wall, hell-bent on shocking him out of his slumber. He said all he wanted was peace. I said all I wanted was poetry that couldn't be put out. And somehow, we both lived to see another day.

By my next decade, I was back in love with another Libra stellium for the ages, whose eyes forever looked through mine to some point on the horizon I couldn't yet see. We boomer-anged back and forth across the planet and across the years. One minute, tucked safely in bed together like the amoebic origin of love. And the next, a voice on the end of the line from California, Bali, India, declaring he'd already packed his bags and moved on. I tried to convince myself that he was shut down and too squeaky clean to face forged-in-the-fire me. But the distance between us was always ours to share.

Wherever I turned, there was a Libra lurking to keep me honest. Libra collaborators who checked my excess. Libra con-fidantes who catalyzed change. Each time I met a new luminary outside of myself, my own Libra Rising sign rose to meet me right back, swinging me across the lines I'd drawn between who I thought I always was and who I believed I'd never be. Through each of Libra's lifts, I learned that I was made from more than what I'd thought of as mine.

Without Libra, I could still be myself. But with it, I could see myself from both sides and then some. The fiery freak who wanted only freedom. The sweet stuffed animal who craved nothing but closeness. The six-years-sober ascetic. The many-more-year substance-drenched stick of dynamite. In Libra's lemon sharp light, I'd chafe at the abrasion of difference as I reckoned with whatever I'd wrecked during the all-nighter the night before. But I could neither deny nor regret what came to its light.

One of my Libra stellium loves once threatened that if I didn't get my shit together and come together, I'd have to go it all the way alone. He menaced me with visions of my end-of-life dead-ending in some single-occupancy hotel, where I'd play back on an endless loop all the Libra loves that had once lined up outside my door. He was almost halfway right.

All the Libra loves still linger in the air. Some of them still show up on the end of the telephone line. But as I stand alone, I find a form of me that isn't made only from friction. A color that isn't visible solely when splashed against a pristine white. From purely defiant, I'm turning consciously oppositional. The exfoliation of sand instead of the scrape of the match against sandpaper.

With a level look, I meet my own Libra Rising face-to-face in the mirror. And I turn toward my own kind of peace, in just the right light.

Beholding Libra: Seeing the Light

To reveal Libra's current, you can start by noticing *how things find their light*—both unveiling the clear contours of reality and heading higher in search of illumination. A stripe of daybreak that streaks across your desk to compel initiation. A leggy plant stretching for sun. A could-be cloud puff in the sky above. Your reach toward the upper shelf to grasp an aspirational object or across the table to clasp hands with a beloved and reconcile the distance.

Next, let the Libra current do its work on you:

Begin by regarding your revelation. The outline of your hands in the early light, peeling back the covers to illuminate each part of your body. Notice how your body wants to see its surroundings. Maybe you tear from the blankets in one sweep and all is clear. Or maybe you choose a considered twist of the Venetian blinds, as little slivers of sun stripe their way into hidden spaces. Imagine that your role is to wake up the entire world to itself. See how you face it. And how it faces you.

Notice the alignment of each thing as it rises to meet its other. Turning the taps in the shower and adjusting the temperature just so, palm to steel. Responding to an early-morning message with the sender in mind and also steady in your own mind as you recount your side of the story.

Without tightening into prescriptive restrictions, see which foods want to come forward and combine in proportions that acknowledge what's right for your body. Consider how your snacks separate and reunite. Strawberries in their bowl and yogurt in its dish, awaiting whipped harmony. Bacon and eggs entering the skillet's shared oil, side by side.

Tailor your measurements to fit the day. Maybe today's a moment to cleave close, with fabrics that curve around your body. Or maybe you need more distance and to find a look that lets the light and air pass between you and your drapery. Curate your contours through a willingness to meet your own materials.

Channeling Libra: Setting Your Sights

From Virgo's last moment-unto-the-self, where we supplicate, in Libra we come together and rise. We are meeting air for the second time. Each layer of the atmosphere moves us farther and farther out from being stuck. In Gemini, we breathe into reciprocity and begin to circulate. And in Libra, we decide our distance and start to elevate.

Libra is **Cardinal Air.** Through it, we are encountering our first **polarity** point (each of the first six signs is partnered across the dance floor with one of the second six signs). Libra's partner is Cardinal Fire sign Aries, and it stares back at Aries' big bang to see how far it has come and how far it has to go. In Aries, we emerge out of nothing, and in Libra, we aspire to something more.

Libra starts our third seasonal trinity of Libra-Scorpio-Sagittarius, where we learn to cross our self-imposed lines and let life run wilder. In Libra, we elevate into the last hours of daylight before Scorpio's nocturne descends, seeing all that we can see so that we can be more of what we could be.

Begin with the parallel sight lines of **Libra's glyph.** A set of well-designed blinds that reveals the hope for harmony that's happening on the horizon. A mutual respect and growing aspiration that emerges from the ground of what's here.

Having faced this symbol, you can then feel for the presence or absence of **Libra planets in your birth chart.** Notice the bright lights and heights where these planets live, and the more obscure spaces that reach for increased clarity.

From here, fan out into Libra's facets by exploring its family of associated planets and cards.

Venus: Your Standard

Venus rules both Taurus and Libra. In its airy expression here in Libra, we shift from absorbing what we desire to lifting it toward the beauty we know it can become. This is Venus as standard bearer and center of value.

To come alive to this expression of Venus, ask yourself:

How do I define what's good, true, and beautiful? What do I aspire to? How do I bring out the best in others and in life? What am I meant to lift up?

Then, you can dive deeper into your own Venus sign and its element, and inquire:

What would life look like if it were designed entirely in this sign's image? How will this sign leave life better than it found it?

You can use these aesthetics for inspiration:

- **Venus in Fire (Aries/Leo/Sagittarius)** *Color*. Elevating beauty that's saturated with life and giving it even more over-the-top, unabashedly "extra" force.
- **Earth (Taurus/Virgo/Capricorn)** *Texture*. Elevating beauty that's tailored to life's innate needs in a given moment and staying close to the grain of what's already gorgeous.
- **Air (Gemini/Libra/Aquarius)** *Pattern*. Elevating beauty that's part of a larger vision of participation and drawing clear lines that lead from reality toward the ideal.
- **Water (Cancer/Scorpio/Pisces)** *Tone*. Elevating beauty that's self-divined and resists definition, and accepting and embracing the greatest range of human forms.

The Rising: Your Face-to-Face

An alchemical front door where we meet life through self and self through life, the **Rising** can only be fully understood along the continuum that includes its opposite sign. Thus, the first polarity pair of signs in the zodiac, Aries and Libra, are its natural keepers. Through polarity, we're reminded that every collision in our life is a chance to reach across the divides within us and around us. Exploring its line of tension lets us live with a more complete picture of self that denies nothing: neither what we turn toward nor what we run from.

To come alive to the Rising, you can start by asking yourself:

What do I believe the world is "all about"? What themes, situations, and kinds of relationships have taught me the most about who I am? Which have confronted me the most?

Then, you can dive deeper into your own Rising sign, considering both this sign and its polarity point. Turn to face both ends of this axis and ask yourself:

How does each of these signs reach for me and under what circumstances? Which of these signs am I coming together with right now? And which am I standing apart from? How can I exist along the continuum between them and embrace both ends of their spectrum as more of my own?

You can use these convocations for inspiration:

Rising in Aries/Libra *The Rally*. Exploring how your growth has been shaped by taking up just causes, cutting away excess, and grappling with consequences.

Taurus/Scorpio *The Banquet*. Exploring how your growth has been shaped by tenacity, retention, attraction, and abiding through cycles of having and losing.

Gemini/Sagittarius *The Festival*. Exploring how your growth has been shaped by improvisation, spontaneity, experimentation, synchronicity, and momentum.

Cancer/Capricorn *The Homecoming*. Exploring how your growth has been shaped by responsibility, protection, belonging, self-sufficiency, and caretaking.

Leo/Aquarius *The Gala*. Exploring how your growth has been shaped by the power of pure presence, essence, expression, and your capacity to hold the room and not lose heart.

Virgo/Pisces *The Workshop*. Exploring how your growth has been shaped by attention to process, environmental sensitivity and subtle signs, and transcendent moments of allowing.

Justice: Your Right Fit

Bolstered by its coruler, the Venus-infused **Empress** card—which grants us the right to receive life's richness—the **Justice** card adjusts this aperture to help us divine what's *for* us on the most fundamental level. This means going far beyond external concepts of right and wrong to lay down our own law. We can use its clarifying properties to acknowledge what must be looked at straight in the eye, to reconcile what we think we want with what actually serves us, and to identify where we must wield Justice's sword to cut the excess and move closer to our truest contours.

When exploring Justice, ask yourself:

How do I define my sense of right and wrong? What codes of conduct govern my life? Where do these spring from, and how do I uphold them?

How do I first notice when something "feels off"? And how do I respond—how do I rectify, readjust, and right things?

What needs to be decided? What is right for me, right now?

Divining Libra: The Art of Aligning

In a world before the arrival of elevated Libra energy, we stand far apart from life. We deny the divisions within us and around us, try to rise above it all and hold humanness at arm's length, and lose hope for a real future by refusing to reckon with what's really here.

At one extreme of Libra energy, we become so dedicated to a rarefied vision of perfected life that we don't deign to live in this one or acknowledge that much of what's here is already doing its best. And at the other extreme, with a lack of all Libra, we stop stretching for the light, shrink our standards, and shrivel our potential.

When wielded consciously, Libra's greatest gift is **the art of aligning**. We exist in relation to whatever faces us by first facing it head-on, then deciding our right distance. Rightness becomes more than an impossible standard we'll never reach and instead emerges from integrating polarities, considering consequences, and reconciling contradictions. Experienced in this way, Libra becomes a balm of conviction, where our highest ideals draw the best and brightest out of each being that's before us.

A Libra future asks us to embrace rectification, reconciliation, and coincidence.

Rectification

We commit to renovating stringent concepts of right and wrong that come from outside us. We advocate for more self-divined forms of rightness that don't deny humanness or chase impossible visions of perfection. When something feels misaligned or off to us, either as individuals or as a collective, we explore how to right it without expending unnecessary energy identifying what "went wrong." Instead, we release judgment and explore how to let each other choose what's truly right for us—which may not be intelligible or explicable to others.

Reconciliation

We honor ourselves as beings who are rife with internalized contradictions and oppositions. While not suppressing anyone's point of view or strongly held beliefs—or the value in friction and opposition—we commit to understanding the intersections that exist between apparent opposites. In this landscape, compromise isn't a denial of difference or of the right to sovereign self-agency. Instead, it is a naturally arising meeting point of shared humanness, where there is always some part of us that is also part of the other.

Coincidence

We look beyond single causes and single effects to explore the interconnected conditions that give rise to actions and reverberations in the world. We become curious about how the less-conscious parts of ourselves are awakened through other people and circumstances. We hold each other accountable for intentions and choices and accept consequences. And we also consider causality within a larger context of co-creative contributions. We release regret by acknowledging that we did what we could with what we had. By affirming that there was no other way here (because here we are), we uncover new ways forward.

Magnetizing + Excavating

Scorpio pulled me down into the swamp with a mattress strapped to my soot-colored station wagon. South, south, south I drove, from the Queensborough Bridge to the Pontchartrain Causeway, as the air turned to stagnant soup on a stick and there was no end in sight. When I showed up to the spot I'd leased, sight-unseen from a scrap of paper on a corkboard, the spectacle was oracular: it looked like the hurricane that would soon hit had already happened.

Pawn shop bars on windows that were as useless as those on the stomach of a steamer. Possums that ate my pasta boxes whole while holed up under the dishwasher. A crazy-eyed crew crashing out on the couch, burning candelabras beside electric sockets gone buzzy blue. A backyard clogged with nocturnal creatures that heaved through the kudzu to have at the trash cans. The whole cinder-block submarine was barely above sea level, just like the city's burial grounds, where the dead surfaced to wring out their sponges.

Surely, this was the edge of hell. And in Aries-stellium style, I swallowed my superhero steroids in one gulp, believing I could battle Scorpio's beasts back onto dry land. My pack of Scorpio Moon co-conspirators kept Nutria rats draining in their fridges for gravy. At Mardi Gras, we'd disappear down to towns where hooded men armed with axes fought on horseback for days to hack the heads off live chickens.

I fell head over heels for a Venus in Scorpio sniper, fresh from Afghanistan, whose side had been eaten by an exploding land mine. When he left because I was "too much," I broke into his house. I didn't even know how I'd gotten inside. I was possessed by some primitive form of Scorpio's ruler, Pluto, which faced off against all the Aries planets in my chart and took me for ride after unconscious rodeo ride straight to Thanatos country.

By the time I saw the cops crossing the front lawn beside another Scorpio Moon lover to tell me my father was dead, I was convinced I was the one being sent straight to jail, charged with some unimaginable fallout from one of my own blackouts. And when the weather forecaster told us that the big storm was coming, I was sure I could hold back a hurricane. While the levees broke and the windows blew in, I fueled my personal mythology of badassery by sleeping in the bathtub alone. Natural disaster was just another notch in my lipstick case of limitless libido. After all, *I* was the only force of nature around.

Back in the five boroughs after my swamp battles, I stacked the death certificates of my family members atop the mounting body count of my sexual conquests, and spat them both back in the face of anyone who'd doubt my ferocity. Sex and death, the domains of Scorpio, were just stories told to shock-jock strangers into more fighting and fucking. In a nasty battle with one catch, they screamed: "You wear your father's suicide like a badge of honor, showing everyone how strong you are!"

But Scorpio was dogged in its desire to cut me closer to its core. The showdown came in the form of a six-foot-seven, three-hundred-pound Aries stellium with a Scorpio Rising. A man so saturated with Mars, just like me, that there was nowhere for our love to go but down into Pluto's underground.

Our battles were brutal. Gaping holes left in hotel walls, and the worst ones of all, those where he'd hit himself in the face to keep from hitting me. With nothing left to push against, my subconscious orchestrated a classic takedown of my crude Aries apparatus. I invited my worst nightmare straight into our bed: a petite Scorpio Sun whose flytrap magnetics made my obvious flex look like a teenage boy's backseat fumbling.

The day my fellow Aries stellium and I broke for good sent me straight to the heart of Scorpio season. November 1. The Day of the Dead. As my stapled-together self-image burned to dust, I was left licking the floor and living with ghosts. In this place of perceived powerlessness, there were no more verbs to action. No noun of me even to upright. Lipstick-less lips. An already sinewy form cut to the bone and ready to roll onto those subway tracks. But I couldn't even summon the force to manage that. Alone in bed, now bereft of any other body beside me, I'd howl like a wolf if any part of my skin brushed against my own skin.

The Scorpio Moon astrologer and therapist who helped me crawl back to the surface of life as a new kind of creature told me stories about Inanna and Ereshkigal. Two Sumerian sisters, one living aboveground and one deep under the dark earth. It turned out I'd been living too long in the light of hot-blooded heroism, and the other sister was hungry for a visit. I'd have to go down, down, down to get back up.

But this wasn't a battle to bring myself heroically back from the brink and claim the dead as fuel for my own life. Scorpio's power couldn't be sourced from the fight against powerlessness. Instead, it had to come from my full body-and-soul pact with all the powers that be.

By Aries season, almost six months after my Day of the Dead, I'd managed to eat some red meat and sit up straight. I booked a flight to the driest land I could locate. And in the blackest night, with no end in sight, I went on foot, down, down, down to the lowest point in the Northern Hemisphere, in the hottest desert in North America.

Badwater Basin, Death Valley.

I stood in the center of that bowl, carved by forces whose hand I couldn't force. Here, in a place even hotter than I was, I was prey for anything. And I had to forgive life for everything.

In that bowl, I had never been smaller. And in that night, I had never burned brighter.

Beholding Scorpio: Drawing It Out

To hone Scorpio's current, you can start by noticing *how things intensify and overturn*. Tree roots growing underneath a cement sidewalk, texturing the surface. A metal detector seeking gemmed glory. Fierce feelings bubbling up and breaking loose. The saturation point of spice in your takeout, possessing your palate. A staring contest with a stranger where you cannot and do not turn away.

Next, let the Scorpio current do its work on you:

Begin in total obscurity. Don't raise the blinds or flip the switches to turn the energy on. Ignite by mining something even deeper. Flex your core muscles around whatever it is you want to hold dear as you face daybreak. Rub your skin vigorously to bring the blood back. Clench and unclench your toes. Grip the bedposts. Push off against the hard parts of the room to find a start so strong that it can let more life in without fearing a leveling.

Notice the way things increase and concentrate. Let your shower run just a little bit hotter or colder than usual. Start with more sweat or more shiver. Hunt through your kitchen to root out the flavors that are fierce enough to face down your hunger. Maybe a measly crumble of granola and nut milk just won't cut it, and you need some pure protein. Maybe your coffee wants to be blacker, thicker, sludgier, more totally itself. Savor the sensations as if your very life depends on it. Because it does.

Dress yourself by first stripping down. In your nakedness, notice the parts of you that pulse. An unwavering eye-lock that wants to be ringed with kohl. Hips that beg to be belted. This has nothing to do with aesthetics and everything to do with baseline charge. It might even be a part of your body that you bristle and balk at. Edge closer and deck out whatever cries out.

Channeling Scorpio: Cutting to Your Core

From Libra's reach up into the light, in Scorpio we head underground. We are meeting water for the second time. Water both possesses us and releases us. Cancer calls us into the safety of our swimming pool. And Scorpio magnetizes us to the bottom of our well and the eye of our hurricane.

Scorpio is **Fixed Water**. All fixed energy fortifies us and fills us with power. Scorpio's polarity partner is Fixed Earth Taurus. In Taurus, we learn to have and to hold. And in Scorpio, we learn to face down fear of loss so that we can be filled by love, again and again. Hunkering down in the center of our third seasonal trinity, in Scorpio we prepare for the expansive freedom of the zodiac's end by uncovering the unmeltable matter that can never be broken, no matter the weather.

Begin with the snake and spike of **Scorpio's glyph**. A penetrative stake. A creature getting its groove. The still center of the storm. A death-defying funnel that feeds life beneath the ground.

Having dug into this symbol, you can then feel for the presence or absence of **Scorpio planets in your birth chart**. Notice the glow-in-the-dark points where these planets glitter and the Scorpio-less spots that crave more of their concentration.

From here, fan out into Scorpio's facets by exploring its family of associated planets and cards.

Pluto and Lilith: Your Power Source

Scorpio's ruler, Pluto, is the first of the outer planets we'll encounter on our journey (Pluto, Uranus, Neptune). Our Sun-Moon-Rising trinity imbues us with being. Through the inner planets of Mercury, Venus, and Mars, we learn to make and do. And through the outers, we get moved and get made.

The entire back half of the zodiac, from Virgo to Pisces, demands that we learn to respond to life out of more than just our fear of death. Each of the outer planets is the "higher octave" of one of the inner planets that we encounter during the zodiac's first half. Pluto takes Mars's live-and-let-live and raises the stakes to die-and-let-live-again. From Aries' emergence, we evolve into Scorpio's resurrection.

Because they move slowly through the signs, these planets act as generational markers (that is, you share the same Pluto sign as those born within anywhere from around twelve to twenty-some years of you). To understand the planets' personal significance in our birth charts, we can explore the little pie slices where they're placed (the astrological houses).

And we can use them to practice going "off chart." The outer planets are the soul schools that wear away our separateness by asking us to confront our perceptions of powerlessness and emptiness. And, as beings who are constantly experiencing evolutionary change, we always exist inside one of their classrooms, whether we're in Pluto's grip and rip, Uranus's clear and sweep, or Neptune's melt and dissolve.

As we move through the three outers in our practice, you can explore your comfort levels with each and divine which style of soul change you might be experiencing in this moment. (You can also isolate their three ruling tarot cards and draw one to help you locate yourself: Pluto's card is **Judgment**; Uranus is the **Fool**; and Neptune is the **Hanged One**.)

When Pluto moves through us, it asks us to give up the fight against whatever feels like the fight of our lives—the place where we experience the strongest attachments and aversions and attempt to exercise the most control. Whatever is in this realm, Pluto demands a reckoning and, until we face it, we'll call Pluto fate. And when we do, we uncover eternal life: the lasting peace and unbreakable core that forges us as a force of nature in fellowship with all forces.

Start by asking yourself:

Where do I experience the most intensity — what incites my most full-on reactions to life? Where do I seek to exert the most control?

What do I fight the hardest to keep alive? And what do I fight the hardest to keep at bay?

When I've "lost" these fights in the past, what have I found within myself?

You can then probe your more personal flavor of Scorpio power by exploring your **Lilith sign**: a birth chart placement that reveals the point in the Moon's orbit where it's farthest from Earth (you can do an internet search for "what's my Black Moon Lilith" sign). Our Lilith sign reveals an archetype we must claim completely so that we're no longer held prisoner by the threat of its unconscious emergence.

As you explore your Lilith sign and its element, you can ask yourself:

What qualities do I disown or disclaim when I see them manifest in others? Which parts of me feel most animalistic, and how can I learn to embrace them?

You can use these creatures for inspiration:

Lilith in Fire (Aries/Leo/Sagittarius) *The Phoenix*. Building power by facing fears about stepping up, standing out, expressing anger, and putting passions on the line.

Earth (Taurus/Virgo/Capricorn) *The Snake*. Building power by facing fears about claiming bodily pleasure,

staking boundaries, following natural urges, and sur-
rendering to life cycles.

Air (Gemini/Libra/Aquarius) *The Eagle*. Building power
by facing fears about not being heard and understood,
unfulfilled potentials, and necessary compromises.

Water (Cancer/Scorpio/Pisces) *The Scorpion*. Building
power by facing fears about being vulnerable, powerless,
and left alone in the undertow of big feelings.

Death and Judgment: Your Life Cycle

These Scorpio cards draw to the surface what is always true: that
the catharsis of change is always happening and that we are a
part of this process. That when we participate more consciously
in our life's cycles, we actually gain power. **Death** invites us to
embrace life's constant composting by camouflaging ourselves
in change. And **Judgment** invites us to welcome the power of
evolutionary pulls and become mightier by responding to the
magnitude of these magnetics.

When exploring Death, ask yourself:

*What "season" of life do I currently find myself within? What
changes are unfolding around me? What changes are unfolding
within me? How can I collaborate with these changes?*

*What is the most natural posture to adopt within my life
right now?*

When exploring Judgment, ask yourself:

*What patterns have powered my life and how have I handled
their pull? What larger forces have interceded in my existence
to "move" me? What do I know that I am here to evolve into?*

What am I trying to change right now that, on some level, I know cannot be changed? And what changes must I make? What more can I take? How can I act as an agent of change on a larger scale?

Divining Scorpio: The Art of Mortalizing

In a world before the arrival of elevated Scorpio energy, we never really know what we're made of because we refuse to test our mettle. Power is something to be seized, strategically and transactionally, and we struggle to stay on top so we don't slide under.

At one extreme of Scorpio energy, we unsettle the surface at any cost: metal-detecting hidden motivations in a calculated ploy to keep the upper hand and have life "out" before it exposes our weakness. And at the other extreme, with a lack of Scorpio, we never move beyond a casual acquaintance with our own existence—hiding out from the high stakes and relinquishing the greatest depth of our love because we refuse to reckon with the specter of loss.

When wielded consciously, Scorpio's greatest gift is **the art of mortalizing.** We embrace our status as animals with appetites and aversions, and we handle more of our humanness head-on and heart-forward. Experienced in this way, Scorpio becomes a balm of unbreakable core power that asks us to grow stronger by giving up our fight against life, forgiving it for its strongest sensations, and bonding with whatever transformation it demands.

A Scorpio future asks us to embrace intimacy, potency, and regeneration.

Intimacy

Whatever life presents to us—however wild, bitter, bright, or sweet—we commit to "going there" with more of ourselves and embracing more of it. We explore fears around losing ourselves to what we love. We excavate what always lives beneath the surface and liberate more of our unconscious obsessions, fascinations, urges, and attachments—even, and especially, the ones we feel are too ugly or too much. We bond with our beasts and become more beautiful together: made robust through our refusal to resist what is most raw and real.

Potency

We give up power moves that are predicated on strategy, comfort, and fears about being too big or too small; instead, we open up to the forces of nature that move through us all. We embrace strong feelings, strong fears, and the big drama of a life that is no less loving for its intensity and ferocity. We help each other through hurt without having to seek retaliation or retribution. We grow power by forgiving each other and forgiving life itself for what it takes from us. We let life demand more of us, and we gain the depth of our love in return.

Regeneration

No matter the conditions, we find it in our hearts to go on. We celebrate each other's resilience and resurrections, and acknowledge that we've all been through our versions of hell and back. We support each other in coming back to life when and how we're ready. We become organic matter by actively participating in the life-death-renewal cycles present in our partnerships, projects, and inner worlds. We expand to embrace a nonhierarchical view of these cycles. We stay curious about the having, the losing, the learning to love again, and every gradient in between. We let die to let live.

9   **Sagittarius**

Venturing + Riding

I sought Sagittarius in the stretch of my
legs along the Strip. Resurrected from the
bottom of Death Valley's Badwater Basin,
there was nowhere to go but Las Vegas.
And to keep going.

Once upon a time, my Aries stellium love and I had tramped
this turf before we imploded. As we sped through the desert
on our way to some bunny ranch brothel, we believed our sex-
tuple serving of Aries combined would somehow add up to the
immortality of Sag.

But it didn't. And I couldn't believe I could face the gaping
hole I'd left here on the Strip. But somehow, anyway and any-
how, when I started crashing through circus tents and levering
wild cherry slots, I stayed up and moved on. Straight into the
larger-than-life dice palaces and never-say-die neon, I rocked
and rolled my body forward and onward.

My legs limbered. My CamelBak sloshed. And my boots punched out Morse code on the pavement. Still here. Still here. Still here. If all of life could, and definitely would, end anyway, my only mandate was to make meaning out of motion. Just keep moving. Just stay up. And of course, in the words of my craps-shooting, blackjack-dealing grandmother, "live it up."

I'd been training for this Olympic-torch form of fire. In that lean, lipsticked libido of my original Aries strut, pounding Jersey beach boardwalks into submission. In the love letters of my Leo Moon's plastic diamond soles, dazzling the patio. And now, in this last of the fire signs — the one where I had only the hope-against-hope far-outer planet of Neptune placed — I walked back from the dead. Each step sent my body past its own predicted demise.

Back in my city, I found that my feet couldn't and wouldn't stop. Heading out to the bodega, I'd suddenly cross three boroughs like some cinematic sprawling vine, taking the whole town with my tendrils. I walked the longest street in each borough. I walked the perimeter of Manhattan. Over every bridge and from LaGuardia to JFK in an afternoon. And when there were no more roads, I hit the tracks, reputedly becoming the first woman to ride the entire subway system in one sitting (32 hours, 17 minutes), armed with only a paper map and a large bag of snacks. In and out of every station on every line, I became a stop-motion kaleidoscope of life begetting more and more life through the opening-closing-opening doors. Floods of early-morning bodies packing themselves in. Almost empty middle-of-the-nights. By the ten-hour mark, my flesh fused with the rhythms, and I rode on and on. Not even a second life in the City of Angels could stop what had been set off. I simply swapped to stronger-soled shoes and performed incomprehensible feats with my feet along the freeways.

Back in the Naked City, my path soon crisscrossed with a group of walking artists, spearheaded by a Sagittarius stellium who spread his steps like promiscuous seed, splashing his meaning-making across the cement with an insouciance that made my Aries stellium feel practically ascetic. We walked backward through a church beside the gaping wound of Ground Zero for a whole day while I wept. We walked silently around single blocks on repeat, as my stories about how things were, or could be, freewheeled into a choose-my-own-adventure.

In anticipation of my Scorpionic breakdown, Sag had already started paving my way, scripting my never-ending story for the moments when I'd lose all meaning. A few months before bottoming out, I'd completed my dissertation, which traced narratives of decline, survival, and renewal in the late 1970s city through acts of taking to the streets. Blackout bodies bursting through Bushwick with boom boxes. Jimmy Carter charting the South Bronx rubble. John Travolta's double-slice disco strut through Bensonhurst. In my quest for higher meaning, Sag had already given me the footnotes for finding my way out.

On that first Day of the Dead, I could barely dress myself. Yet, somehow, I showed up upright for my first ever astrological walking tour—a service I was calling Street Signs, where I'd lead people to city sites that would bring their birth chart energies to life. From the center of a sardine-packed Queens cemetery, I guided a man along the spiced sidewalks of Jackson Heights, urging him ever closer to his Sagittarius Moon's free range. Next up, it was a Scorpio Sun on the Coney Island boards, where we stood side-by-side next to the empty place where the Thunderbolt rollercoaster had once been. In its material absence, we summoned the spirit of a rumble.

As I moved through the streets, I had no idea how far down I'd have to go. Or that the same subway that had sent me to near-Guinness-book glory would mutate into the weapon beside which I'd death-fantasize my own finale.

I couldn't know, by design, whether I would ever reach any place other than this one. But Sagittarius knew the whole time. And with each stride against cement, I placed my bets and kept the beat. Side by side, Sag and I forged faith through every footstep. Ride or die.

Beholding Sagittarius: Setting It Off

To seek Sagittarius's current, you can start by noticing *how things let loose and head on their way*. A foot-off-the-pedal coast down sloping terrain. A jar lid gallivanting across the countertop. A squirrel going nuts on a magic mission up a tree. A fledgling plan that becomes more freewheeling as you let your mind run wild. Pay attention to how backing things with your belief allows them to grow bigger and go farther.

Next, let the Sagittarius current do its work on you:

Begin in unkempt sprawl. Maybe hit the snooze one too many times and show up a little late. Maybe leave the sheets in an unmade pile. Know that you don't have to get it together to get started. Let any lingering signs of sleep roll off your back as you roll out of bed.

Pay attention to the trails. How do you get from the bed to your next locale? Where are the signs of life from last night?

Explore the topographical map of your existence heretofore and the course you're now charting.

Once you're up and at it, head outside immediately. Whether or not your mane is combed or your contacts are in or your robe is cinched, let the world encounter more of the unedited and uncut magic of you. Notice how wild ways spill out of things. A shout on the street corner. The skid of tires. The burst of a morning jam that doesn't monitor its sound level.

Take your breakfast al fresco, on the back patio or fire escape, or at the corner café. Assemble a smorgasbord-style selection, spreading leftovers and found foods out on the table. Leave the dishes in the sink.

Dress yourself for both kinesis and celebration: travel-ready and party-ready. Stay in this immediate moment, forgoing strategic designs while you go through the closet. Put on more and more of what appeals, costume-trunk style. See what sticks and what slips off throughout the day. Leave whatever slips behind you as you go as sartorial signs of your ongoing adventure.

Channeling Sagittarius: Shooting Your Shot

From Scorpio's face-down with death, in Sagittarius we give life another go with all that we've got and rock and roll toward every last reason to live.

We are meeting fire for the third and final time. In fire, the only imperative is existence. We are given the birthright of our being in Aries. In Leo, we magnify into beings only we could be. And in Sag, we find immortality: exhuming evidence of the ongoing adventure of aliveness anywhere and everywhere we find signs of life.

Sagittarius is **Mutable Fire**. All mutable energy accompanies us as life unfolds. Sagittarius's polarity partner is Mutable Air Gemini. If Gemini is the subtle gesture, Sagittarius becomes the sweeping motion. We let life breathe through us in Gemini, then in Sagittarius, we let it run wild.

Sag closes out our penultimate seasonal trinity. As we prepare to barrel toward the end of the astrological year, the momentum of its burn must be enough to get us all the way back to Aries on the other side.

Begin with the see-if-it-sticks spirit of **Sagittarius's glyph**. A shot in the dark. A freewheeling flare that finds its course. A celebration of charge. A flag of forever onward and upward.

Having gambled on this symbol, you can then feel for the presence or absence of **Sagittarius planets in your birth chart.** Notice the spots where these planets stretch their legs and the places without them that long to come unshackled.

From here, fan out into Sagittarius's facets by exploring its family of associated planets and cards.

Jupiter: Your Good Faith

Sagittarius's ruling planet, Jupiter, serves as a gateway between the more personal inner planets and the evolutionary forces of the outers. Jupiter offers us risk tolerance: the chance to believe in the benevolence of something bigger. When we embrace it, life gets luckier. Not because our existence is all love and light or endless jackpots, but because loosening our grip on the checks and balances helps us get more out of whatever our gods give us. If everything eventually ends, says Jupiter, we may as well follow it to every possible end.

Start by asking yourself:

What are my definitions of winning and losing? How do I handle it when things turn out differently than I imagined? How do I believe the world "works"? And what do I need in order to believe that life is on my side?

Then, you can dive deeper and explore your own Jupiter sign and its element. This planet is the law of your personal cosmos, and you can use its energy to build trust that life is only ever unfolding *for* you, far beyond the binary of good/bad fates.

Ask yourself:

How would it feel to just go with this sign and its element —running off behind it without a second thought? What would its wildest form look like? What does life mean when viewed through its lens? What would a world lived according to its credos look like?

You can use these guides for inspiration:

Jupiter in Fire (Aries/Leo/Sagittarius) *Spirit of the Law*. Believing in a world of high-highs, where life carries you through the peaks and valleys if you're willing to just keep coming courageously back at it with your lights still on.

Earth (Taurus/Virgo/Capricorn) *Law of the Jungle*. Believing in a world of organic rhythms and integral nature, where life carries you surely on its back and responds according to your appetites, abilities, and innate capacities.

Air (Gemini/Libra/Aquarius) *Letter of the Law*. Believing in a world where all happenings are both "just happening" and also adding up to an interconnected understanding, where life carries you through shifting perspectives and inspires ongoing conversation.

Water (Cancer/Scorpio/Pisces) *Law of Love*. Believing in a world of invisible currents and inexplicable intrigues, where life remembers your heart and returns you to the right place when you let yourself loosen into loving.

The Wheel of Fortune and Temperance:
Your Way and Your Why

These Sagittarius cards ask us to let life take us farther and to allow each move we make to make a meaning of its very own. In the **Wheel**, we let life find its own way: we keep things in motion and divest our attachment to knowing exactly where it's all going or how it will get there. And in **Temperance**, we let life find its own "why" by agreeing to embark on the adventure of our lifetime and opening to a larger story about what our existence really signifies.

When exploring the Wheel, ask yourself:

How are things moving right now? What do I believe is deciding the course of events?

What outcomes am I expecting? What actions do I believe will create these outcomes? How could I be open to more potential ways through my situation?

When exploring Temperance, ask yourself:

How do I search for significance and find meaning in experiences, especially in moments that appear to be devoid of it?

What is the bigger picture and larger purpose of what I'm experiencing right now? What is my "why," and how can I give myself over to it more completely?

Divining Sagittarius: The Art of Chancing

In a world before the arrival of elevated Sagittarius energy, we claim our credos with zealous blind faith and run recklessly in the name of our so-called freedom.

At one extreme, we become meaning-making maniacs who are so fanatical about our never-ending search for significance that we can't keep a promise or find a home. And at the other extreme, with a lack of Sagittarius, we're petrified to throw down the gauntlet and quest after our wildest "whys," and we lose all possible benevolence in the embittered belief that we were born to lose.

When wielded consciously, Sagittarius's greatest gift is **the art of chancing**. We back our beliefs while staying open to see what actually sticks, al dente style. And we forge our faith by increasing our chances: moving through more of life so that it invariably gives us more of its good stuff. Here, Sagittarius becomes a footloose balm that joyously sloughs off the too-small strictures of safety, makes meaning in motion, and finds faith that more life is always on its way.

A Sagittarius future asks us to embrace kinesis, dynamism, and fortune.

Kinesis

We commit to diversifying our ways through the world and challenging linear trajectories. This means keeping things moving and contributing our energy, even when we don't know exactly where something might be going. And it means giving up certainties and assurances of given outcomes in the name of increased risk and possibility. We set things off and see where they go, and then we give it another go. We recognize different rates and qualities of movement and momentum, and celebrate the wild ways in which we keep our spirits up and carry on.

Dynamism

We commit to untamable truths by exploring both how we've come to our beliefs and worldviews through specific experiences and how these can alter through other experiences. We interpret and understand life as it meets us, and open ourselves to the spontaneous, unpredictable, on-the-fly, and unprepared. We let things grow, expand, and seek in their own style and according to their own reasons. We send each other on our own ways in the quest after our own whys, and celebrate our seeking without having to find it, fix it, or stick to the so-called facts.

Fortune

We challenge the concept of luck as either a finite, fated amount of goodness given out by a random universe or as a hard-earned prize to be won through work. Instead, we embrace optimism and the pursuit of joy as an unflagging force of change in a deeply unfair world. We support each other's risk tolerance levels in accordance with the conditions and contexts that have contributed to our chances of achieving success. And we commit to multiplying everyone's chances by taking more chances together. We forge faith by leaving space for life to surprise us. And we grow our faith when it does.

Claiming + Weighing

Capricorn laid its relics at my feet. At our family's home wakes, we stuffed our open caskets with bottles of brown liquor, packs of playing cards and poker chips, and the most point-worthy Scrabble tiles. The spirits and divining rods of our inheritance, all close enough for embalmed hands to grasp. Beside the coffin in the living room, one of the grown-ups would inevitably pass out cold, flattened by their grief. And beside them, little kid me would spread my tarot cards, bearing witness to a life legacy that was both bound to a box and beyond it.

Through the years, Capricorn became my skin cream, sharing its hard-won secrets through time-release as I lived into each line in my face. As a wild young thing, I fetishized it through alpinist love interests, chasing anyone who could brave their body against bedrock. Like its polarity partner, Cancer, Capricorn was "intercepted" in my chart, disappearing without a doorway. And for all my metaphorical fire, I couldn't even start one with two sticks. So I'd stand at the base of the boulders like some would-be wartime widow and pray for the survival of my paramour. The most majestic of all was the Capricorn mountaineer. When the two of us reached our end, he presented me with an album that memorialized our era. *One day, you'll understand*, he said, as I railed against the limit. *Give it time*.

I thought I could counterfeit my solid ground through these survivalists, but my own Capricorn had to be earned. During my Saturn Return (Saturn is Cap's ruling planet), it told time through my bones. Deep into my doctoral exams, I woke to find all my joints mysteriously calcifying, grinding against one another with every move I made. I'd spent the better part of the previous thirty years behaving like I didn't even have a body. Boozing and drugging into oblivion. Walking for twenty miles on a whim in shoddy shoes. Fucking any body for sport. And now Capricorn froze me so that I could feel the finiteness of form. When I quit trying to find out the medical meaning of this motionlessness and stopped to stand exactly where I was, the pestling of my matter ceased.

Each decade Capricorn's gravity became more insistent, and as I entered my forties, it sent my many lives banging against the back of my body like a highway pileup. It all started with the Cancer season flood that dredged the archives. I'd never really believed in time. Or believed it could end by anything other than my own design. And now here it was: all the matter I'd made with my hands and my heart, turned to mashed and pulpy paper. Capricorn's tree rings telling their own tale as old as time.

As a kid, I'd experienced vivid episodes of spatial intuition — able to seize the full stories of the heavens and hells that unfolded within houses simply by standing on their foundations and feeling their walls. And now, after the flood, a portal to the past appeared, and I was sent back to inhabit all the lands I'd left behind.

I bailed a teen diary from the drink and out slipped a letter I'd penned to a boy I'd idolized at age fourteen and never sent. Days later, after almost thirty years, he appeared through an internet message, saying I had come to him in a dream. We found ourselves together on a bench in a childhood park with aging hands and the same old hearts, and I finally handed the bubble letters over to him.

An attempted trip to Cairo turned impossible, and I was routed through connections in cities where I'd smeared my youth with a glitter pen, never believing the pink ink would end. Upon my return, I was sent straight back to the ancestral home of all those family wakes to sit atop the peeling white rock at the edge of the yard where Mom Mom used to wait in her housecoat with her whiskey for the kids to come home. And after more than a year of trying in vain to obtain tickets to see a beloved pop star perform all her "eras," a friend's husband suddenly had a plus one. The locale: New Orleans. The spot I hadn't set a foot in since I'd fled a form of Scorpio, post-Katrina.

The high tide had turned back time. And there was no other way forward but to turn and face it. On this midlife haunted-house tour, I was accompanied by my closest friend, an Aries Sun with a Capricorn Moon. Together, we showed up to stand before the sites of our lives. The intactness of some of these structures was shocking. The same graffiti splash across the door that led to the room where the divorce was finalized. An instinctual turn that revealed the very same tiny gold church where a cluster of nuns had once encircled another version of us in bands of light.

I was here, we whispered to each other. *It really happened, I swear*. The bones of these buildings had been here the whole time, and our bodies knew the way back. But our own bones were no longer entirely the same. As we walked our past out across the empires, my twenty-mile-per-day, never-say-stop fire feet developed their first ever bunions.

And then, as my bunioned feet snaked slowly down an alley onto a slip of Parisian street called the "Road of Virtues," the full weight of Capricorn hit the cage of my chest. This was the site of the one-room apartment with the broken toilet where I'd once lived with the Capricorn mountaineer. The man who now lived at an altitude that made my head throb and my nose bleed. And whom I knew I would never live with ever again in this lifetime.

Hundreds of mes had run down this street, forever in forward motion. And now here I stood, still. With the lines in my skin and a boulder at my back, Capricorn and I had been waiting for this me all this time. We caught her in our arms as she ran. And we showed her, by the very fact of our bones, that there were no roads but all the roads that had led from there all the way back here.

Our final stop on what we'd now coined "The Grandevous" was the grave of my Cap Moon friend's great-aunt, in a village tucked between two Tuscan lumps. This great-aunt was the one who'd been left behind in Italy as a child. Shrouded in the brocade of family lore, she was known chiefly through the cinnamon color of her hair and her scratchy pink cardigan that no one else could wear. Unwed and without children, just like her, my friend and I had begun to channel her existence into a line of artifacts we constructed. Fabrics that could have held her. Plates that could have fed her. An oracle deck where she spoke firmly from the seat of the beyond.

We found her bones stored high above the ground in a sliding drawer in a cemetery the size of a broom closet. We climbed to reach her, teetering from the top of a rolling metal staircase that we pushed over uneven stones. We'd been told she was a Sagittarius Sun. But there it was, her birthday etched into the marble in barbed black licorice: January 12. A Capricorn.

The final card of our oracle deck—the one that maps to the World card in the tarot, ruled by Saturn—bears her face and her name.

There is no other life, it reads. *There was no other way. All of this is all yours.*

We laid it down beside her slab and left it.

Beholding Capricorn: Keeping Time

To honor Capricorn's current, you can start by noticing *how things weatherize*. The patina on outdoor furniture as it faces a colder shift in the elements. A bone stock that matures into a complex flavor profile on the stovetop. Explore letting things around you be in, and of, their time. The weight of waking from dreams of a past partner. The familial jut of your chin, inherited from another's angles.

Next, let the Capricorn current do its work on you:

Feel into the downward current that already exists when you awaken. And see what it actually takes to get you up against it. Maybe you lie there for an hour, motionless. Maybe you spring into action, avoiding any suspicion of stillness. Just notice how you stack yourself. Explore this small act of bodybuilding from which everything else will grow.

As you move around the room, consider what it's all resting on. The space where you stand. The building where you live. Dig more cavernously into your chair. Or take a constitutional around the block and observe everything that's stuck "in" and "down." The tentacles of trees. The foundations of structures. How they root and how they reach and how each begets the other.

Once you're upright, consider what would fortify you for the long haul. Maybe it's a chocolate spread, straight from the jar. Maybe it's the tarry sediment of Turkish coffee. Maybe it's nothing at all. Whatever your appetite, consider what it will take to sustain you.

In the Northern Hemisphere, Capricorn marks the dawn of winter, when our clothing must consolidate and protect us. Whatever your hemisphere, consider a strong silhouette. A haute high waist. A timeless scent. Choose forms that both tailor to your shape and cut shapes through space. Don't shy away from dense drapery, sharply defined shoulder pads, bangles worth their weight. Leave a wake through the world in your reinforced container.

Channeling Capricorn: Earning Your Keep

From Sagittarius's immortalizing ride into the sunset, Capricorn paves the road as far as it goes: making what's most meaningful into solid matter, giving grit to our glory and persisting until the end.

We are meeting earth for the third and final time. In Taurus, we embrace the beauty of a body and all that it can touch and taste. In Virgo, we bow to this body in its specific constitution. And now, in Capricorn, we prepare to leave our body behind in the relics of our bones.

Capricorn is **Cardinal Earth**. All cardinal energy gets out in front of life to confront and protect. In this final cardinal sign, we initiate our closing season of life at peak performance, in the prime of our lives. All the way from Aries' cardinal act of creation, we've matured into the last moves that we'll make.

Capricorn's polarity partner is Cardinal Water Cancer. Cancer returns us to the liquid conditions of our birth and Capricorn stacks our bones. Here, we claim what we've inherited and build what's born to last from what we've been granted.

Begin with the maturity of **Capricorn's glyph.** The challenge of tracing its hard-candy and cave-aged curves. The stamina for the final ascent. An elaborate signature for a package of exquisite quality, sealed with velvet ribbon.

Having earned this symbol, you can then feel for the presence or absence of **Capricorn planets in your birth chart**. Sense the spots where these planets stand the test of time and the places without them that want to be given more of their ground.

From here, fan out into Capricorn's facets by exploring its family of associated planets and cards.

Saturn: Your Maturation

Alongside Jupiter, Capricorn's ruling planet, Saturn, serves as a gateway to the evolutionary forces of the outer planets. Saturn is where our spirit heads to the gym, and it grants us the points of resistance that build our resilience. Anything Saturn touches, it wants to make more real. When we practice this planet, we face up to whatever we're up against in this lifetime: the tangible limits, the time-based lessons, and the legacy work we're meant to live out.

Start by asking yourself:

What's always been hard for me? What am I up against? What matters most? What's still here? And how will I go on?

Then, you can dive deeper and explore your own Saturn sign. This planet is your personal aging process. It is the wisdom that comes from your willingness to work it, and it's how you will wear this work and weatherize through time.

Ask yourself:

What confronts me about this sign and its element? How has my relationship to it matured and changed over time? What might it long to leave behind—and how does it deposit its residue? What am I bringing to an end in this lifetime through my work with it?

You can use these ages as inspiration:

Saturn in Fire (Aries/Leo/Sagittarius) *Age of Innocence*. Tracing all the rises-to-the-occasion that it took to get you here. The courageous flexes. The bold forces. The history of a heart on the line.

Earth (Taurus/Virgo/Capricorn) *Rock of Ages*. Tracing all the times you took life on and made something out of it. The resilient roots. The lines in skin. The steady composure, bearing down and staying with.

Air (Gemini/Libra/Aquarius) *New Age*. Tracing all the times you've been able to reinterpret what you've inherited and loosen its hold on you. The shifting patinas of perspective. The limits that were lifted. The pasts that parted to reveal other ways forward.

Water (Cancer/Scorpio/Pisces) *Coming of Age*. Tracing all the time-after-times where the past has echoed through you. The time travels that have tenderized you. The stories you've borne. And how you've become time's confidante and keeper.

The Devil and the World: Your Gravity

These Capricorn cards invite us to take fuller ownership of our lives. In the **Devil**, we slough off the weight of the world, learning to exercise our inner authority and call our own shots without shame. And in the **World**, we claim our weight: confronting the finite fact of grand finales, embracing the entirety of our experience, and deciding what we'd like to leave behind from our existence for the earth to inherit.

When exploring the Devil, ask yourself:

What do I answer to? Where does the seat of my authority reside? Who or what do I believe calls the shots?

Where do my "shoulds" come from? Which ones are inherited from my lineage or culture? What do I believe will happen if I deviate from these shoulds?

What part of my life or myself would I like to own more completely? How can I begin to claim this part as part of my turf?

When exploring the World, ask yourself:

What feels heavy right now? Where does this heft come from—how much of it is mine to bear and how do I want to hold it?

Which courses in my life have culminated? Which doors are closed? How can I honor this finiteness?

How am I contributing to the legacy I'd like to leave? What do I want to put my weight behind? How can I bring my lifetime of experience to bear on what's here?

Divining Capricorn: The Art of Prevailing

In a world before the arrival of elevated Capricorn energy, we let life's hard work harden us: we calcify into conservatism and enforce boundaries that keep life out without owning our inner dominion. At one extreme of Capricorn energy, we become taut, rigid, and dry, aging into brittle narrowness. And at the other extreme, with a dearth of Capricorn, we lose all backbone, becoming formless figments who refuse to claim our stake and bear our weight.

When wielded consciously, Capricorn's greatest gift is **the art of prevailing**. We encounter the rough stuff and let it cut us into diamonds. And we welcome this weatherizing process as the gateway to a wisdom that treasures the high quality that can only come through time. Here, success doesn't stack up hierarchically. Instead, it expands horizontally: we earn our tree rings, and we share what we've earned and learned, growing up together because our base is sturdy. Experienced in this way, Capricorn becomes a pro-aging balm, where we wield life's gravity with grace and give it what we've got for as long as we've got.

A Capricorn future asks us to embrace sovereignty, lineage, and caliber.

Sovereignty

We restore our rightful roles as keepers of our own wise counsel and protectors of this planet. This means dismantling patriarchal, paternalistic, and hierarchical orders of control, and transforming dominance into dominion: taking the sovereignty over our lives that strengthens our turf from the inside out, rather than having to police the edges to keep the outside out. Boundaries spring from a natural sense of inner belonging. In deciding what's best for ourselves, we liberate others to locate their own wants, shoulds, and musts. Thus, we uphold an order that embraces each of our capacities to hold ourselves upright.

Lineage

Without over-valuing age as the sole marker of worth or wisdom, we celebrate the long line of lives that has led to ours. We acknowledge what these lives have brought to bear on us and the responsibility we have to make something out of this inheritance. While recognizing the need for divergence, we also honor what endures. We celebrate the maturation process as one where we decide what we must carry, what we can't carry, and what wants to carry on. Our legacies live at the intersection of all that's lived before us, all that's lived through us, and all that we long to leave behind.

Caliber

We embrace experiences that build our bones and cut our teeth, and we stay spry as we weatherize. We identify standards of excellence that both acknowledge our limits and also stretch our muscles to capacity. Sometimes, we bear more than we think we can take, and we let this weight evidence our virtuosity instead of becoming a burden. We use pressure to produce creations of inarguable quality. And we give ourselves the time and tenacity it takes to become worthy of our own works of art.

11   Aquarius

Witnessing + Envisioning

From thirty thousand feet up, Aquarius both terrified and fascinated me. Seen through the oval window of the jumbo jet, the personalized compact of Leo color I held so close turned to nothing but beige geometry. From up here, all of life was "just happening" down below. And it wasn't just for me.

It started on my first flight to ancient Greece, at age three, prancing down the aisles with my My Little Ponies in tow, only to turn violently ill as we took to the blue. By middle school, it had become a full-blown obsession. Clutching tiny airplane talismans to my neck like rosary beads, from takeoff to touch-down, I whispered elaborate spells from my window seat. Because surely, only I could keep all this metal up. The possibility that anything other than my own divinations could determine my destiny meant instant death. Back on solid ground, I kept binders of smudgy plane-crash newspaper clippings, donned flight attendant costumes for Halloween, and spent birthdays at Philly International's rooftop parking lot, just to catch a glimpse of the underbelly of those fearsome hovercrafts.

And then, at age fifteen, with my jet black bob bent over my plane chains, I was given a different vision. On takeoff between two Brazilian cities, the same old terror sharpened my sight. Flight attendants seemed to float just off the cabin floor, already turned ghostly. I searched for any sign that our destined-to-doom lives would be saved. The smile of a passenger I knew couldn't leave life just yet. The magic ding of a seatbelt sign turning off. The remains of a salted snack package: the few nuts saved for later as evidence that life later on would still happen.

And then, as the slow-mo got even slower, suddenly it struck me. A knowing that arrived complete and intact: I had died here before, so I wouldn't again. Back home, having survived the flight, I scoured the local library's card catalog for records of commercial crashes, convinced that locating my birthday in another year was the key to cracking my phobia. After two full days spent in the stacks, with my silver airplane charm still banging against my chest, I finally found it: the one crash that had happened on April 12, more than a decade before my birth, on a commuter flight between the same two cities in Brazil. There had been no survivors.

On the countless flights to come, I'd shudder and sweat just the same. But I knew I could no longer keep us passengers aloft with my witchy whispers. I was just a cloud poof, part of a larger pattern. Perhaps a bit rosé in my tone. A personalized pink, Care Bear kind of cloud. But a "just happening" just the same.

At first, I had mistaken Aquarius's great wide open for a lack of affection and had resisted its efforts to unstick me from the land that I loved. This wasn't Gemini's breeze bopping me along in ballet class. Or even Libra's about-face light of day. Aquarius's midwinter midtown wind tunnels existed far beyond my opinion. They sent my body banging against the sides of buildings as I kicked and punched against the invisible rush of air with my fists and my feet, trying in vain to determine my own course through the streets.

But Aquarius was everywhere. It had broadened me as I played along the Leo–Aquarius axis, crafting heart-shaped imaginary worlds that could hold it all with my successive line of Aquarius Sun and Moon best friends. It had shocked me sober on a crystalline morning in early February, Aquarius season, when I awoke to the same hollow head and thick tongue, and gave up drink on the spot, out of the icy blue. And it had rushed my body off the side of the mountain in Rio (where, yes, I'd made it in one piece), hang gliding me straight into the groundlessness of my worst fear of flying. And instead of trying to mastermind it, I let the wind take me and toss me like I was nothing at all.

Finally, it came in the form of an Aquarius stellium friend-turned-lover who came out of nowhere. Our union was an empty room. A grand respect that expected nothing and held nothing back. This Aquarius stellium saw all the assembled mini mes from miles away. Before Aquarius's untroubled regard, my many selves blew right through me and, suddenly, I could be anyone. The wind tunnels I'd fought with my fists had only ever wanted to free me. To scoop me into a stillness of self that could hold anything and anyone.

And when I found myself on one of the rockiest flights of all, heading back from an Aquarian edge of the world in Big

Sur, I scoured the plane for something to hold, stalled in that same-old phobic slow-mo. But then I saw it: a familiar flash of fear in my seatmate. As the metal pitched and jolted through cloud cover, I grasped the hand of this stranger–neighbor and didn't let go. And when I stilled my panic enough to bear witness to the panorama around me, I saw that all the other humans were doing just the same. Strangers. Lovers. Children. Parents. Way up here, we were all hand-in-hand as we hurtled out of and back into the widest blue.

Beholding Aquarius: Opening Space

To electrify Aquarius's current, you can start by noticing *how things make, take, and hold space*: renovating what's stuck, tapping out from circumstance to connect to their own intelligence, and welcoming more of what arises into their expanse. The alive silence after a storm tears the sky in two. Arriving out of a thicket into an unexpected clearing. Letting the intensity of emotion simply land and settle in your field.

Next, let the Aquarius current do its work on you:

Start by staying in stillness for a second. Before you rush to fill the air that surrounds you with your own charge, pause to take in the panorama. Enter the scene of what's unfolding outside your window as a loving witness. Watch these sights and sounds and smells that began their motion while you were sleeping. Know that they will continue, with or without you. But that they want you here to hold them, all the same.

Crack a window. Crack the fridge. Crack a can open. See what portals you can puncture. Consider nourishment that leaves room in you for speculation and interconnection. Maybe it's imagining the foodways your snacks traveled to arrive here, and how they're passing through on their way elsewhere. Picture yourself from above and imagine the similar kitchen table tableaux unfolding across your country and around the world.

Buff and scrub your body, then stand in front of the mirror before clothing yourself. Take in the blank-slate reality of you, cleared and clean. Who you are at your most absolute, without masking. Notice both how you look like every body, and how your view looks like no other, seeing what only you can see.

Consider clothes that will take you from here to wherever your "there" is. Interchangeable, neutral pieces that can take in without having to hold too fast. Spacious enough to create a little extra room in whatever rooms you enter.

Channeling Aquarius: Widening Your View

Through Capricorn, we decide what lasting legacy we'll leave. And now, in Aquarius, we learn to bear witness as we unstick from earth. We are meeting air for the third and final time. All air energy wants to see where things go, both launching it toward ideals and liberating its possibilities. In Gemini, we catch a sliver of breeze that multiplies life's forms. In Libra, elevation reveals the shaft of light where we aspire to greater life. And in Aquarius, we commune with the entirety of existence under the width of the whole sky.

Aquarius is **Fixed Air**. This is the stillness of space and the visions that arise from this vastness. Like all fixed energy, its call is doubled: an interplay between absence and presence, empty and full. As the final fixed sign, Aquarius empties us to our fullest absence. And because of this breadth, there are no limits to what Aquarius can then absorb. From its capacity to look beyond whatever is before it and to neutralize its response, the boldest biodiversity is born.

Its polarity partner, the Fixed Fire of Leo, asks us to be the heart. And Aquarius asks us to see to the heart: unveiling the innate intelligence in all forms of life and letting this interconnected knowing reach more hearts.

Our final seasonal trinity of Capricorn-Aquarius-Pisces marks the moment where we surrender to invisible machinations. It is the end of the astrological year, when we are no longer given direct evidence of futurity, so we must learn to trust in what we cannot see or touch.

Begin with the even charge of **Aquarius's glyph**. Constant current straight from the socket. Libran horizon lines gone rogue. A heart monitor witnessing the waves. Eccentric creatures creating in tandem.

Having widened into this symbol, you can then feel for the presence or absence of **Aquarius planets in your birth chart**. Explore both the spaces where these planets open and the more constricted corners in need of clearing.

From here, fan out into Aquarius's facets by exploring its family of associated planets and cards.

Uranus: Your Void

As one of the outer planets, Uranus wants to move us. Its predecessor, Pluto, uproots. And Uranus clears the debris, hoovering any clogged areas of consciousness and lifting us clean out of one way of being.

With a sweep and a swoosh, this planet hollows us out so that we can hold even more. By harnessing its energy, we learn both how to consciously orient toward the openings in our lives and how to handle the unimaginable clearings that come through us without any warning signs.

Start by asking yourself:

Where do I want to make space? From what do I need to take space? And how can I hold more space for what's happening here?

What kind of oracle am I? When I release the need to know, what do I naturally know about the way it's all going?

Aquarius energy asks us to hold our own place within the whole. Uranus moves through each sign about every seven years, and we can use it to understand seven-year cycles, based both on our own Uranus sign and in communion with the sign where Uranus currently sits.

Explore both your own Uranus sign and where we are collectively in our Uranus cycle (just search online for "What sign is Uranus in right now?") and ask yourself:

How can I use these signs to see beyond what's here? What would it feel like to be cleansed and cleared by them? How can I open to their style of storm medicine?

You can use these weather patterns as inspiration:

Uranus in Fire (Aries/Leo/Sagittarius) *Temperature*. Witnessing how hot or cold your current life conditions feel, and letting the relative temperature inform how much bareness or buffering you might need to weather the storm.

Earth (Taurus/Virgo/Capricorn) *Pressure*. Witnessing how light or heavy your current life conditions feel, and letting this relative pressure inform how you hold on to what matters and give up what's meant to go.

Air (Gemini/Libra/Aquarius) *Wind*. Witnessing how fast or slow your current life conditions feel, and letting this relative wind speed inform how you move with change and catch its current.

Water (Cancer/Scorpio/Pisces) *Precipitation*. Witnessing how wet or dry your current life conditions feel, and letting this relative precipitation inform your emotional response: either power-washing to gain perspective or letting even more feelings pour forth.

The Fool and the Star: Your Renovation

These Aquarius cards invite us to broaden our horizons and restore our inner vastness. In the **Fool**, we give things space: emptying ourselves of expectations and anticipations, defamiliarizing ourselves with the rote, and unearthing the fundamental groundlessness that lives under even the most solid-seeming of grounds. And in the **Star**, we take our place: resetting, recovering, and restoring the natural order of our lives and our original essence within them.

When exploring the Fool, ask yourself:

How do I handle the unfamiliar? What feels overly familiar? How can I open myself to more of the unfamiliar within this familiarity? What wants to be emptied of expectation?

What do I know that I fully embrace? What do I know that I might not want to know? What don't I know that I fully embrace? What don't I know that I really wish I did?

When exploring the Star, ask yourself:

What wants to be restored, reset, and repaired in my life right now? What pieces want to come together? What no longer has a place?

What fundamental forms and original truths lie beneath all the accumulated layers of my life? Who is the "original" me, and how can I hold more space for this being?

Where am I in space right now, and where is my place? When I reach a still point, what can I see about myself and my life?

Divining Aquarius: The Art of Clearing

In a world before the arrival of elevated Aquarius energy, we refuse to see beyond what's present. By clinging to the known at all costs, we lose our capacity for grand visions beyond what's been, and cut off our evolutionary potential by refusing to welcome the aberrant and idiosyncratic as expressions of life's endless biodiversity.

At one extreme, with an excess of Aquarius, we beam so far into the future that we lose heart, playing with the panorama of life like a pack of pawns. And at the other extreme, with a dearth of Aquarius, we get so stuck in our singular dramas that we can't pan out our view, forgetting that it's all just happening in the name of a much bigger heartbeat.

When wielded consciously, Aquarius's greatest gift is **the art of clearing**. When something arrives, we cultivate curiosity about its provenance and trust its providence. And when something is gone, we rest in the gap and let mystery give rise to our next move. Experienced in this way, Aquarius becomes a prescient balm that lets us bear witness with loving detachment and use our vision to understand our place in life's bigger plan. Here, we trust that we'll know what we need to know, when and how we'll need to know it.

An Aquarius future asks us to embrace observation, divergence, and prophecy.

Observation

While we honor the force of feelings, we also let them swirl and settle to see what truths bob to the surface beneath our initial reactions. We cultivate a tender regard, but from a place of witnessing, where our level of direct emotional involvement does not have to be taken as evidence of the strength of our love. We take a long and wide view of life, and see where employing a "just happening" approach can actually reveal the interconnections among these happenings and how they contribute to a very human whole. In holding a wider space for what's before us, we naturally start to see beyond it.

Divergence

We embrace the aberrant, the strange, the sudden, and the unexpected—not just as emblems of individuality or singular deviation, but as evidence of our emotional evolution into more life-forms. We pay attention to the outliers and follow them out to the edge. And we help each other embrace our edges: the beliefs and ways of being that are just beyond our current consciousness that we can't always see or act on by ourselves. We support a biodiversity of being wherever we see it: a greater range of emotional responses, actors, identities, and outcomes.

Prophecy

We diversify our modes of intelligence and ways of knowing. We celebrate the innate, distinctive intelligence that is present in every form of life on earth and in life-forms that have moved beyond life into death. We help one another to embrace our knowns, our not-yet-knowns, and our ultimately unknowables, and to confront the mysteries of life in our own mysterious ways. We embrace revelations and visions that don't have to be understood to be believed. We imagine worlds other than this one, no matter how far away they seem.

Pisces

Allowing + Releasing

All the way out on the island, at the place they call "The End," Pisces came for me at last.

I followed the beach road in familiar funeral garb. Black roses twisting up the backs of my tights. My usual magenta mouth flashing in the foggy early March morning like a lipstick lighthouse. From the Jersey boards out to Montauk, I was still here in my heat. Following the specter of a strut across the spun sugar of misted sand.

At first, this particular Pisces season had been all echo. In the language of astrocartography, which maps birth charts onto globes, this latitude and longitude lit up for me. I'd been to these precise nautical coordinates before. For a friend's weekend birthday bash where I ducked behind the dunes to swallow the bitterness from the Libra stellium's latest departure. For the last summer with the Aquarius stellium—to this place where he'd been born to a fisherman who trawled the deep—in a Virgo season when I bowed my head to the humid dusk of nature's change. And it was here where the Aries stellium had reputedly wed the Scorpio I'd invited into our bed. A whole life of big dogs and lobster rolls spreading out before them, with me nowhere to be found within it.

Apparently, this was the place I was sent to leave my love. But this time, as I let it slip through my hands, I could only keep on loving through the leaving.

The dearly departed was a Virgo Sun who had blinked in and out of my life for years. Emerging together again months before his unexpected death, on our late-night psychic hotline we poured poems into each other without limit, like teenagers clutching the cordless. We incanted all the way back to the beginning. His first childhood poem was called "The Sun Is On." Mine was titled "Mail Me." Two mini-missives that turned our hearts on and let them loose.

Our relationship resisted incarnation. From my Aries to his Virgo, we leapfrogged all the way to the Pisces end of the line. Each time it was time to meet in the flesh, he couldn't make it past the bodega to board the train from Jamaica, Queens. Caught inside the tsunami of his mind that had led him to lockup after lockup as they tried to medicate his multitudes. And for the first time, after all my fucking and fighting and forcing carnation, I found that the flesh didn't matter any more. I loved him just the same through the ether. Maybe even better.

And then, sudden silence. After a month of no more messages, I dreamed of his death and woke to find it. An obituary notice for the next-day funeral led me to the fathomless pews of a Catholic church at the end of this island for a ceremony where I knew not one other soul.

Along the route, there had been a sweet scattering of signs. A medium session booked hours before the discovery of his sudden absence without "knowing" why. A cat named Rupert, wide-eyed and otherworldly, awaiting me on a motel welcome mat. Half-dreams where all my dead circled the king bed and spoke themselves back into being through my tongue.

I was his last stop for love while he was on this side of life. And as I stepped out onto the sands, I faced the sea alone.

No poetic translations or pop songs on the wind. No soft bend of seagrass parting my way. There was only and solely the width of the world's emptiness. The gaping without-ness of a land with one less in it.

As I stood into the wind with my lipstick still on and my low-heeled boots sinking into the sand, here it was at last. The solar Aries mission I'd always thought had to be fought for and won. But which could only ever be received by letting life use me, however it wished, as fuel for its own continued fire. I'd been so hung up on the Pluto force headbutting all the Aries planets in my chart that I'd almost forgotten that all that Aries energy "trined" Pisces' ruler, Neptune, too—a relationship in astrology that's like a chaise that wants to be lounged on, a gift waiting to be unribboned.

And now, Pisces was asking me for everything so that I could come from nothing again. A heroic dot on this horizon whose existence becomes evident only because it dares to disappear.

One day, the ocean will claim all that there is of the places we've been. Even this one.

So what else can I do but let it begin?

Beholding Pisces: Slipping Away

To get carried away by Pisces' current, you can start by noticing *how things love through loosening*—fading, melting, fusing, and befriending impermanence. Slowly turn down a dimmer switch. Perceive the subtexts and secret gestures in conversation. Notice the space just before you fall asleep. Turn butter into béchamel. Watch a friend recede into the distance after a meetup.

Next, let the Pisces current do its work on you:

Stay in the slipperiness of still-almost-asleep. Slowly lift your lids then let them close once again, mixing the images behind your eyes with the ones in front of them. As you come to "real" life, notice the parts of your space that might look like your dream. And how, perhaps, what you thought you'd left stable last night may have shifted in the room. Maybe, just maybe, things are not wholly what they seem.

Melt into matter without forcing yourself to materialize. Leave a snail trail of blankets behind as you move from the bed. Keep your bathrobe on and the lights low. Find nourishment that slides into your body without your having to crunch or chop. Experience a warm sip of beverage or pliable bite as the fusional taking in of something that wants to reunite with you. There is no separation between substances.

Get dressed without trying to see. Without the full-length mirror or the brightly lit vanity. What do you feel like today? Who do you feel like? Catch a glimpse of yourself only in passing. Consider coverings that are almost ready to slink. So the breeze could lift your skirts. So a lover could undo the buttons with only one look.

Channeling Pisces: Undoing Your Effort

In Aquarius, we widen to hold the width of the world. And now, in Pisces, we are here in this wide world for the last time. Looking out at our lives through the eyes of leaving lets us learn to love without limit. We hold each creature in our gaze for a final goodbye, and we invisibly enter its energy, eroding the barriers between us so that we can linger with the sweetness a little longer.

We are meeting water for the third and final time. Cancer brought us in, encircling us. Scorpio drew us down, excavating us. And, finally, we let Pisces carry us all the way out, evanescing us. All water offers us intimacy with the inexplicable and the invisible. It is a remembrance, a return, and a release of resistance that asks for our forgiveness. In Pisces, we forgive the grand finale and let this reconciliation release us into the infinite.

Pisces is **Mutable Water**. Gemini breathes us. Virgo bends us. Sag runs us wild. And Pisces undoes us. Pisces' polarity partner is Mutable Earth Virgo. In Virgo, we distill the divinity from every dot and become digestible. And in Pisces, we are imbibed by the divine: surrendered to our status as dazzling specks and ready to disappear into a sea of stars.

All roads lead to Pisces. It is the current that courses under everything. Each sign travels toward it and must learn to let go through it. Because in the end, Pisces will come for each and every sign.

Begin with the leave-and-linger of **Pisces' glyph**. Two pool noodles bound yet buoyant. Catch-and-release netting. Curved bodies in bed. The seal on a letter saying a long goodbye.

Having dissolved into this symbol, you can then feel for the presence or absence of **Pisces planets in your birth chart**. Notice where there is slipperiness and where there is solidity. The Pisces planets that are longing to leave, and the places without them that resist being left behind.

From here, fan out into Pisces' facets by exploring its family of associated planets and cards.

Neptune and Chiron: Your Hope Against Hope

Pisces' pair of celestial bodies both render us wholly human and help us transcend. When we let them through us, we learn to forgo our need to fix and we *feel with* instead. The far outer planet Neptune is our heart's greatest hope: where we're invited to loosen our logic and sacrifice tangible security for fuzzy-edged fantasies and saving grace. In the trinity of outer planetary change, Pluto uproots, Uranus clears, and Neptune dissolves.

Because Neptune moves so slowly through the signs, we can access a more personal form of Pisces' current by tapping into our Chiron sign. Alongside Neptune's greatest hope, Chiron offers us our greatest hurt: a soul-deep spot we fear we might never get to touch in this lifetime. Both Neptune and Chiron serve to sensitize us. They exist beyond effort and ask only for our acceptance. In return, they give us our empathetic connection with all of life's longings.

Start by asking yourself:

What do I hope for more than anything? How can I embrace this longing, whether or not it's fully met through the world? And what is my deepest hurt? What common root joins this hope and this hurt together?

What does acceptance look like for me? What does release feel like?

Then, explore your own Chiron sign, and ask yourself:

What would it mean to soften into this sign and its element during moments of heartache? What do both wishing and wounding look like when touched by it?

You can use these forms of forgiveness as inspiration:

- **Chiron in Fire (Aries/Leo/Sagittarius)** *Redemption*. Allowing life to become freer through your forgiveness. Seeing where setting things loose and letting longings live could bring more autonomy. Letting hurts and hopes be expressed and exposed and the heat of your heart shine without shame.

- **Earth (Taurus/Virgo/Capricorn)** *Absolution*. Allowing the "shoulds" to soften. Seeing where sloughing off the penances and lifting weights of responsibility could bring more stability. Giving hurts and hopes to the ground, then watching them sink down and give way for more life to be found.

- **Air (Gemini/Libra/Aquarius)** *Amnesty*. Allowing the context for acceptance to become wider. Seeing where blamelessness creates spaciousness and how panoramic perspectives could bring more peace. Letting hurts and hopes be carried away, and reimagining and reinterpreting their original charge.

- **Water (Cancer/Scorpio/Pisces)** *Mercy*. Allowing gentleness to build resilience. Seeing where giving over and going with both the wishing and the wounding could bring more closeness. Harboring hurts and hopes safely, then sending them out to sea to learn how to swim.

The Hanged One and the Moon: Your Multitudes

These Pisces cards invite us to meet multiple versions of reality and embrace the melted movements of a nonlinear life. In the **Hanged One**, we surrender stringent progress, submit to circumstance, and let things come together and come undone all on their own. And in the **Moon**, we let ourselves become lost in a séance of self: carried out into the inexplicable, the uncanny, and the echoes within us.

When exploring the Hanged One, ask yourself:

What's not yet complete? Where am I longing to move on? And where might I be hanging on? In either state, what other realities might I access by releasing into my current conditions?

How can I distinguish between different realms of doing: what wants to be consciously acted on and done; where am I being asked to enter a state of non-doing; and what can I allow to come undone?

When exploring the Moon, ask yourself:

What haunts me? What overwhelms me? What feelings are most familiar—echoing through me from either my earlier life history or from unknown sources? How do I handle these uncanny and inexplicable aspects of self, and how can I connect with this realm more vibrantly? How can I immerse myself more fully in the mystery?

Divining Pisces: The Art of Losing

In a world before the arrival of elevated Pisces energy, we are destined to live and die as flesh and bone alone. Our existence is made solely from the sticks and stones we can scrape together solo, and we're so determined to come from nothing that we lose our connection to everything.

At one extreme, with an excess of Pisces, we are spineless sponges who soak up the world's hurts with no sense of self. And at the other extreme, with a dearth of Pisces, we never learn how to love: so caught up in staking our spot and keeping it all together that we remain forever far apart.

When wielded consciously, Pisces' greatest gift is **the art of losing**. We acknowledge that all of life is always slipping away. And when we learn to look through the lens of these loosenings, we look through the eyes of love, at long last. Experienced in this way, Pisces becomes the boundless balm for all our separateness. When we allow existence to ultimately evanesce, going its own way, which is the way of all life, we become no different than every speck of dust. And all the more dazzling for the divinity that comes from our willingness to disappear.

Here we are, with the world as it's always longed for us to be. In the place where every particle is proof of the presence of god.

A Pisces future asks us to embrace immersion, impressionism, and the infinite.

Immersion

We come together with whatever comes for us. This means learning when to forgo the hard lines and strong opinions and to fuse into experiences that erode the edges of our identities and challenge our sense of specialness. We value complete embraces over partial inclusions. Trusting in the singularity we've experienced by grace of moving through every other sign of the zodiac, we can now become atmospheric: existing as willing participants who no longer fight for our right to be here or fight to hold back any corner of our hearts. We plunge into the pool of life without limits and let ourselves disappear to become part of divinity.

Impressionism

We let life affect us, move us, and change us, continuously and irrevocably. While honoring both our hurts and our desires to heal, we no longer force each other to try and fix things, get over it, or move on. We celebrate the spirals and circles of life, and support one another as we soul search and move through our emotional work in our own style and time. We let our bodies and spirits bear the marks of this life, and we recognize that we are all marked. We cannot ever understand what each of us has gone through to be here. And so we tread as lightly as we can through our lives, finding the face of god in every being we meet.

The Infinite

We forgo overreliance on the provable and the finite and come alive to magic. This means elevating empathy over explanation and challenging the divides between the real and the unreal. We no longer use accountability, action, or actuality as the sole measures of meaningful connection. In whatever forms grant each of us more freedom, we open to the séance of ourselves: the communion where the dearly departeds, the disappeared, and the diaphanous are alive and well inside of us and all around us. We stop trying to orchestrate the endings and let life, and one another, come and go. When something appears, we embrace its wonders. And when it evaporates, we embrace it as no less here.

ACKNOWLEDGMENTS

To all those I've loved with, lost with, and come back to life again beside: thank you for giving off your glow, from all sides.

Special thanks to the wisdom and wildness of Shirley Rigby, Abigail Molotsky, Miles Richardson, Elaine Peña, Lanie Kagan, Lindsay Mack, Maria Soledad, Sandy Sitron, Sue Hunt, the Witches Without Kids coven, Zach Fredman, Zivar Amrami, Justin Ritchie, Bridgette Trezza, Cara George, Elizabeth Ault, Margret Grebowicz, and the Duke University Press team. And to the works of Liz Greene, Dane Rudhyar, Alejandro Jodorowsky, Alana Fairchild, and Niki de Saint Phalle.

And, always, to the infinite lives of the dearly departeds summoned within these pages: John Paul Matassa, Kathryn Rose "Missy" Healy, Philip Healy, Quinn Boley, Otea Maria Pollera, and Jesse Jordi Domenech.

www.ingramcontent.com/pod-product-compliance
Lightning Source LLC
Chambersburg PA
CBHW021404090426
42742CB00009B/994